Movie-Based Illustrations
for Preaching & Teaching

4/22

Movie-Based Illustrations for Preaching & Teaching

101 Clips to Show or Tell

Craig Brian Larson & Andrew Zahn

Editors of *Leadership* & PreachingToday.com

GRAND RAPIDS, MICHIGAN 49530 USA

ZONDERVAN™

Movie-Based Illustrations for Preaching and Teaching
Copyright © 2003 by Christianity Today International

Requests for information should be addressed to:
Zondervan, *Grand Rapids, Michigan 49530*

Library of Congress Cataloging-in-Publication Data

Larson, Craig Brian.
    Movie-based illustrations for preaching and teaching : 101 clips to show or tell /
Craig Brian Larson and Drew Zahn.
       p. cm.
    Includes bibliographical references.
    ISBN 0-310-24832-9
    1. Homiletical illustrations.   I. Zahn, Drew.   II. Title.
BV4225.3 .L36 2003
252'.08—dc21

                                      2002156682

Interior design by Todd Sprague

Printed in the United States of America

03 04 05 06 07 08 09 /❖ DC/ 10 9 8 7 6 5 4 3 2 1

Contents

Introduction. 9

1. Acceptance
   Toy Story 12

2. Adultery
   Hope Floats 14

3. Affirmation
   Hoosiers 16

4. Affirmation
   Renaissance Man. 18

5. Apology
   The Legend of
   Bagger Vance. 20

6. Backsliding
   The Matrix. 22

7. Baptism
   The Piano 24

8. Bible
   The Hurricane. 26

9. Brokenness
   Star Trek V 28

10. Calling
    Dead Poets Society. . . 30

11. Caring
    Patch Adams. 32

12. Challenges
    Hoosiers 34

13. Christ, Substitute for
    Humanity
    Beauty and the Beast . . 36

14. Christ, Substitute for
    Humanity
    The Lion King 38

15. Community
    I Am Sam. 40

16. Community
    With Honors 42

17. Complacency
    Dead Poets Society. . . 44

18. Confession
    Dead Man Walking . . . 46

19. Conscience
    Roman Holiday. 48

20. Consequences
    Groundhog Day 50

21. Convictions
    Chariots of Fire 52

22. Convictions
    The Remains of
    the Day 54

23. Courage
    Dead Poets Society. . . 56

24. Dedication
    The Patriot. 58

25. Dependence on God
    The Inn of the
    Sixth Happiness 60

26. Determination
    Remember the Titans . . 62

27. Discipline
    Shrek 64

28. Discipline
    Uncorked. 66

29. Dreams
    A Christmas Story . . . 68

30. Enemies
    Ruby Bridges 70

31. Evangelism
    Gettysburg. 72

32. Example
    Mr. Holland's Opus . . . 74

33. Experiencing God
   The Preacher's Wife . . 76

34. Faith
   Apollo 13 78

35. Faith
   Contact 80

36. Faith
   The Empire
   Strikes Back 82

37. Faith
   Indiana Jones and
   the Last Crusade 84

38. Faithfulness
   Mr. Holland's Opus . . . 86

39. Fatherhood
   The Parent Trap 88

40. Fatherhood of God
   Field of Dreams 90

41. Fear
   First Knight 92

42. Forgiveness
   The Mission 94

43. Friendship
   It's a Wonderful Life . . 96

44. Generosity
   It's a Wonderful Life . . 98

45. Gospel
   Amistad 100

46. Grace
   Pay It Forward 102

47. Hardship
   O Brother, Where
   Art Thou? 104

48. Heaven
   Annie 106

49. Help from God
   The Legend of
   Bagger Vance 108

50. Human Worth
   Schindler's List 110

51. Injustice
   Glory 112

52. Integrity
   The Devil's Own 114

53. Integrity
   The Legend of
   Bagger Vance 116

54. Jealousy
   Amadeus 118

55. Kindness
   Pay It Forward 120

56. Kindness
   Sandy Bottom
   Orchestra 122

57. Leadership
   Remember the Titans . . 124

58. Leadership
   U-571 126

59. Love
   Addicted to Love 128

60. Love
   The Hurricane 130

61. Love
   Tuesdays with
   Morrie 132

62. Marriage
   Family Man 134

63. Marriage
   Father of the Bride . . 136

64. Mentoring
   Finding Forrester . . 138

65. Mercy
   A Christmas Story . . 140

66. Mercy
   Les Misérables 142

67. New Life
   Air Force One 144

68. Parenting
   Jack Frost 146

69. Peace
   Bonhoeffer: Agent
   of Grace 148

70. Peace
   The Shawshank
   Redemption. 150

71. Perception and Reality
   The Matrix. 152

72. Planning
   Fiddler on the Roof. . 154

73. Pleasing God
   Chariots of Fire 156

74. Prayer
   Shadowlands 158

75. Providence
   Simon Birch. 160

76. Purpose
   Antz. 162

77. Racism
   Cry, the Beloved
   Country. 164

78. Reconciliation
   Remember the Titans . . 166

79. Reconciliation
   The Straight Story . . 168

80. Reconciliation
   The Straight Story . . 170

81. Redemption
   Les Misérables 172

82. Redemption
   Toy Story 2. 174

83. Regret
   On the Waterfront. . . 176

84. Secrets
   City Slickers 178

85. Seeking God
   Contact. 180

86. Selfishness
   Rules of
   Engagement 182

87. Selflessness
   Princess Diaries . . . 184

88. Self-Worth
   Princess Diaries . . . 186

89. Servanthood
   First Knight 188

90. Significance
   Requiem for a
   Heavyweight 190

91. Sowing and Reaping
   Mr. Holland's Opus . . 192

92. Strength
   Ruby Bridges. 194

93. Success
   Field of Dreams 196

94. Temptation
   It's a Wonderful
   Life 198

95. Temptation
   The Lion King 200

96. Temptation
   Pinocchio. 202

97. Transformation
   As Good as It Gets. . . 204

98. Trials
   Snow Dogs. 206

99. Truth
   Yentl. 208

100. Unbelief
   The Red Planet 210

101. Wrestling with God
   The Apostle 212

Scripture Index. 215
Keywords Index 223

Introduction

Movies have become the literature of our culture. Listen in on the conversations going on around you in a restaurant or at the mall, and you will hear people discussing the latest movies they've seen. Movies, therefore, are one bridge we can walk in order to connect with hearers where they are. Like literature, they offer a vast array of scenes, situations, and stirring stories (exactly what preachers crave)—things that preachers and teachers cannot always get from their personal experience. Movies are a treasure-house of metaphors and phrases. Mention a movie in a sermon, and watch everyone turn a listening ear.

Aware of this, in early 2001 PreachingToday.com began including movie illustrations in our weekly batch of ten new illustrations provided to our online subscribers. This book gathers the first seventy-five movie illustrations in our database—and then adds twenty-six illustrations that have never appeared on our site.

Each illustration includes relevant Scripture passages and multiple keywords that are thoroughly indexed at the beginning of each entry. Each also gives a brief statement on the content rating of the movie. Even if you never see the movie yourself, you have what you need to draw an illustration from it.

You do not have to show the movie clip in order to use these illustrations. We have written these in a way that assumes the movie clip will not be shown—providing necessary plot summary and describing the crucial scene concretely—but we have included elapsed times so that those who do show the clip can easily find the scene.

Avoiding the Objectionable

How do we decide which movies are worthy of drawing out illustrations? In this book we do not illustrate from any movie regarded as having no redeeming value. In addition, we do not illustrate with any scene that contains objectionable elements (in other words, we illustrate from some PG-13- or R-rated movies, but we use no PG-13- or R-rated scenes).

The illustrations in this book, therefore, do not use scenes that contain profanity, because we want preachers and teachers to be able to show a clip during the message if they choose to do so. If some objectionable element in the movie immediately precedes or follows a selected clip, we include a warning.

How to Get Copyright Permission to Show Movie Clips

Do you need permission to show movies (even short clips) in church? *Yes* (though permission is not needed just to tell the illustration). You could argue the "fair use" copyright rule for using snippets of movies for sermon illustrations—that's what allows preachers to quote small portions from books and articles—but the safer and more ethical approach is to purchase a license.

The licensing system works a lot like the CCLI license that many churches purchase in order to print or project song lyrics. In fact, Christian Copyright Licensing International (CCLI) has recently partnered with Motion Picture Licensing Corporation (MPLC) to offer a service especially for churches. Church Video Licensing International (CVLI) offers an "umbrella license" for an annual fee. You can show authorized titles from MPLC's long list of big studios (including Sony, Warner Brothers, and Disney) and from a growing list of Christian movie producers. This license covers clips in sermons, plus videos shown in classes and youth groups and at events such as family film nights—as long as no admission fee is charged and the title is not advertised to the general public.

Fees are based on church size: $150 for churches with average attendance up to five hundred, $200 for churches above five hundred. Smaller churches can license only the religious titles if they wish—$45 for churches with average attendance under one hundred, $75 for under two hundred. Licenses can be granted over the phone, just in time for your next sizzling sermon illustration or Sunday night's Billy Graham film. Contact Christian Video Licensing International at 1-888-771-CVLI (2854)—on the Internet at www.cvli.org—or their sister organization, Motion Picture Licensing Corporation, 5455 Centi-nela Avenue, Los Angeles, CA 90066–6970 (on the Internet at www.mplc.com/), by e-mail at info@mplc.com, or by telephone at 1-310-822-8855 or 1-800-462-8855.

Craig Brian Larson
Editor, PreachingToday.com

1. ACCEPTANCE

Toy Story

Topic: *Belonging to God*

Texts: *Isaiah 43:1; Isaiah 44:5; Romans 8:14–17*

Keywords: *Acceptance; Attitudes and Emotions; Family of God; Fatherhood of God; Identity in Christ; Meaning of Life; Self-Worth; Significance*

In Disney's animated movie *Toy Story*, Woody (a plush toy cowboy) confronts Buzz Lightyear (a toy astronaut) with the fact that he is only an action figure and not really a space hero. Early in the movie Woody shouts, "You're not a space ranger! You're an action figure—a child's plaything."

Only after failing to fly does Buzz realize the truth of Woody's statement. Grief-stricken and disillusioned, Buzz hangs his head in resignation, declaring, "I'm just a stupid, little, insignificant toy."

Woody later seeks to comfort his friend by underscoring the love of the boy who owns them both. "You must not be thinking clearly. Look, over in that house there's a kid who thinks you're the greatest, and it's not because you're a space ranger; it's because you're his."

As Buzz lifts his foot, he sees a label affixed to the bottom of his little shoe. There in black permanent ink is the name of the little boy to whom he belongs. Seeing the image of his owner, Buzz breaks into a smile and takes on a new determination.

Elapsed time: Measured from the beginning of the opening credit, this scene begins at 00:56:54 and goes to 00:59:31.

Content: Rated G

Citation: *Toy Story* (Disney, 1995), written by Joel Cohen, Alec Sokolow, Andrew Stanton, and Joss Whedon (from an original story by John Lasseter, Pete Docter, Andrew Stanton, and Joe Ranft), directed by John Lasseter

submitted by Greg Asimakoupoulos, Naperville, Illinois

2. ADULTERY

Hope Floats

Topic: *Devastation of Adultery*

Texts: *Exodus 20:14; Deuteronomy 5:18;*
2 Samuel 11–12; Proverbs 6:27–29;
Malachi 2:13–16; Matthew 5:27–28;
Matthew 19:4–9; Romans 13:8–10;
1 Corinthians 7:10–16; Hebrews 13:4

Keywords: *Adultery; Betrayal; Children; Commitment;*
Faithfulness; Family; Fatherhood; Fathers; Happiness;
Marriage; Men; Rejection; Selfishness; Sex; Sin; Ten
Commandments; Unfaithfulness; Vows; Women

The 1998 movie *Hope Floats* is the tale of a woman struggling to recover from her husband's infidelity. It shows how she and her child cope with the problems caused by the breakup of their family.

The mother, Birdie Pruitt (played by Sandra Bullock), thinks she's going to receive a makeover on a national TV talk show, only to discover that the real purpose of the program is to uncover her husband's affair with her best friend. Horrified, Birdie returns to her small-town Texas home and tries to pull life back together for herself and her daughter. While there, she faces considerable obstacles and the potential rebirth of an old high school romance.

Toward the end of the movie, Birdie and her husband are arguing loudly in front of their daughter about the pain, deceit, and anger his adultery has caused. She tells him, "I would have stayed with you forever. I would have turned myself inside out for you!" But Bill won't hear it. He says he's finally found happiness for himself, and he's going to take it.

Finally, Birdie tells him to leave since she's got the best part of him anyway, namely, their daughter, Bernice. Bill turns to go and is pursued by Bernice down the stairs and out to the car. She calls out, "I'm coming with you, Daddy!" but her dad keeps walking to the car. The girl, terrified of losing her father, tries to get in the car with him, begging, "Daddy, I need you!"—but he refuses her.

He says sternly, "I promise to come back for you, but I am starting a new life with Connie now."

As she screams and sobs, his raised voice has an empty ring to it, as he keeps repeating, "I promise, I promise, I promise." With that he drives off, leaving Bernice completely devastated, wailing until her mom comes and lifts her up into her arms.

This clip captures the heart of what God tries to spare us from when he says, "You shall not commit adultery."

Elapsed time: The scene from the beginning of the argument until the car drives off lasts four and one-half minutes; it begins about one hour and forty minutes into the movie.

Content: Rated PG-13 for two vulgar jokes and mild profanity

Citation: *Hope Floats* (20th Century Fox, 1998), written by Steven Rogers, directed by Forest Whitaker

submitted by Bill White, Paramount, California

3. AFFIRMATION

Hoosiers

Topic: *Taking Risks on Others*

Texts: *Matthew 25:14–30; Matthew 28:18–20; John 3:16; John 21:1–17; Romans 8:31–32; 1 Corinthians 4:1–2; 1 Corinthians 12; Ephesians 4:11–16; 1 Timothy 1:12–14; 1 Peter 4:10–11*

Keywords: *Affirmation; Church; Encouragement; Faithfulness; Fear; Growth; Ministry; Responsibility; Risk; Second Chances; Spiritual Formation; Spiritual Gifts; Stewardship*

The movie *Hoosiers* tells the Cinderella story of a small-town Indiana high school basketball team that wins the state championship. One important character, an alcoholic named Shooter (played by Dennis Hopper), has failed at most things in his life—but he has an extraordinary knowledge of and passion for the game of basketball.

The coach (played by Gene Hackman) works with Shooter to give him a second chance in life. He asks Shooter to be his assistant coach, and soon Shooter is on the bench.

The little-known Hickory High School basketball team is starting to experience winning ways when, during a pivotal game, the coach decides to get himself thrown out. He pulls the referee aside and says, "Take me out of the game." The ref doesn't know what the coach is up to, but he tosses him from the game.

Shooter is terrified. A few scenes earlier, after another drinking binge, Shooter promised the coach he'd stay sober and remain as the assistant on one condition: "You've got to give me your word," said Shooter, "that you will not be kicked out of no games!"

The end of the game is near, and the score is tied. The Hickory players call a time-out. In the team huddle, all eyes are on Shooter—including his son's, who never thought his dad should be in this position in the first place. Shooter is paralyzed by fear. He can't speak. Finally his son says, "You reckon number four will put up their last shot, Dad?" That seems to jump-start Shooter, and he haltingly calls a play. The team goes back on the floor and begins to execute it, when Shooter calls another time-out.

Now he is completely engaged in the game, and his knowledge and passion for basketball have overtaken his fear. He lays out the strategy for the next play with confidence: "All right, now listen to me. This is the last shot we got. All right? We're gonna run the picket fence at 'em. Merle, you're the swingman. Jimmy, you're solo right. All right, Merle should be open swinging around the end of that fence. Now, boys, don't get caught watchin' that paint dry!"

The players are with him. They walk back onto the court, run the play to perfection, and sink the game-winning basket. Of course, Shooter and the players are deliriously happy. Amid the celebration, Shooter's son looks into his father's eyes and says, "You did good, Pop. You did real good."

A weak, shame-filled alcoholic accomplished genuine good because the coach decided he was worth taking a risk on. In the same way, God sees our value and loves us enough to take a risk on us.

Elapsed time: Measured from the beginning of the first visual of the movie, this scene begins at 00:55:57 and goes on for two minutes and thirty-five seconds.

Content: Rated PG

Citation: *Hoosiers* (Hemdale Film Corporation, 1986), written by Angelo Pizzo, directed by David Anspaugh

submitted by Elaine Larson, Barrington, Illinois

4. AFFIRMATION

Renaissance Man

Topic: *Believe in Me, Daddy*

Texts: *1 Corinthians 13:7; Ephesians 6:4*

Keywords: *Affirmation; Children; Encouragement; Family; Fatherhood; Fathers; Love; Parenting*

In the movie *Renaissance Man,* Danny DeVito plays a middle-aged divorcé named Bill who has lost his job. For the first time in his life, this man with a master's degree from Princeton experiences the humiliation of standing in line at an unemployment office. His teenage daughter, Emily, who loves astronomy, asks him to pay for a class trip to Mexico to see a once-in-a-lifetime eclipse. Since she lives with her mother, she does not know he has lost his job.

In one scene, Bill and Emily are at Tiger Stadium watching a base-ball game. Emily again asks about the trip to Mexico and says she wants to pursue astronomy as a career.

Bill sneers, "Oh, there's the path to big bucks—staring out into space. Oh, look! I discovered Venus! Pay me." He continues on. "Astrology," he suggests. "Maybe you could make a few dollars telling people's horoscope or something."

Emily says, "Why do you always have to be such a jerk about all of this?"

In the next scene, Bill drops off his daughter at her home. As she stalks away from the car, he goes after her. "Em, wait a minute! Em, come on!" he says as she walks away. "I'm sure we'll find a very nice eclipse to see around here sometime."

"Yeah," she responds, "in the year 2047!"

Waving her souvenir pennant from the game, he pleads with her one more time, "Do you want your pennant?"

As she slams the door, she responds in a wounded voice, "No. I just want you to believe in me."

Caution: Immediately before this scene, while at the game, Bill uses the name of Jesus in vain.

Elapsed time: Measured from the Cinergi studio logo, this scene begins at 00:09:59 and ends at 00:10:41.

Content: Rated PG-13 for profanity

Citation: *Renaissance Man* (Touchstone, 1994), written by Jim Burnstein, directed by Penny Marshall

submitted by Debi Zahn, Sandwich, Illinois

5. APOLOGY

The Legend of Bagger Vance

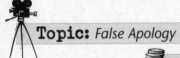

Topic: *False Apology*

Texts: *Matthew 5:25; Acts 26:20; Ephesians 4:31–32; Titus 3:2*

Keywords: *Apology; Confession; Conflict; Faultfinding; Forgiveness; Pride; Reconciliation*

The Legend of Bagger Vance tells the story of a promising young golfer, Rannulph Junuh (played by Matt Damon), who loses his "swing" because of the emotional trauma he suffered in World War I. Years after the war, he returns to his native Savannah, Georgia, to squander his life with gambling and drinking. His ex-girlfriend, Adele (played by Charlize Theron), invites him to play in a historic golf match with two golf greats, Bobby Jones and Walter Hagin.

Halfway through the match, Junuh is dogged by his past and can't hold his game together. He falls a daunting twelve strokes back after the first round of eighteen holes. All of Savannah is disappointed in his poor play.

Adele comes to apologize for snaring him in this embarrassing situation. The humorous scene accurately portrays how most of us resolve conflict.

When Adele sits down next to Junuh on a bench, he questions, "There something you wanted to tell me?"

Adele responds, "Well, I'm trying to think of how to say it, Junuh. There is a purpose to this visit. The purpose is to apologize. But I'm not actually an apologetic woman, so it takes me a little longer to get my thoughts in order. I wanted to seem properly contrite for getting you into this golf match, but not seeming that what I did was ill-intentioned, because it was not."

Confused, Junuh probes, "So what exactly are you apologizing for?"

Adele confesses, "For publicly humiliating you."

"Well, that would be a good thing to apologize for," remarks Junuh.

But Adele's pride overcomes her, and she reneges, saying, "However, I think basically that what I'm trying to say is that I'm sorry, but it's not my fault. You're the one to blame."

At the end of this scene, there is a long pause, and Junuh comments, "That's one hell of an apology, Adele."

Editors' Note: We've chosen to leave this final quote in to reflect the rendering in the movie clip. We did deem it important that you be aware of the potential offense to certain hearers, and then to leave it to your judgment as to whether you use the full clip as is or edit it as you see fit.

Elapsed time: Measured from the beginning of the opening credit, this scene begins at 01:06:30 and lasts approximately one minute and fifteen seconds.

Content: Rated PG-13 for some sexual content

Citation: *The Legend of Bagger Vance* (DreamWorks, 2000), written by Jeremy Leven (based on a novel by Steven Pressfield), directed by Robert Redford

submitted by Bill White, Paramount, California

6. BACKSLIDING

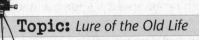

The Matrix

Topic: *Lure of the Old Life*

Texts: *Matthew 10:28; Romans 6:16–23; 1 Corinthians 15:19; Ephesians 4:22–24; Ephesians 6:10–18; James 4:4; 1 John 2:15–17*

Keywords: *Backsliding; Comfort; Convenience; Evil Desire; Expedience; Old Man; Perseverance; Satan; Sinful Pleasure; Spiritual Warfare; Temptation; Truth; World*

The Matrix is a science-fiction movie in which computers (called the Matrix) take over the world. The computers keep their human slaves in bondage by plugging wires into their minds and creating for them a false reality. The humans think they are free, but they are actually entombed in little pods where the computers feed off their energy.

A few humans have escaped and are battling the machines, but life is hard in the real world. Instead of the dreamland of the Matrix, the world is full of sweat and stress and combat with the computers at every turn.

In one scene a human named Mr. Reagan (played by Joe Pantoliano), who knows the truth and has spent nine years on the side of freedom, considers going back over to the side of the Matrix. Even though he knows it's not the real world, it is an easier life.

Sitting at a table in a fancy restaurant, Reagan negotiates with a computerized agent about the decision. The Matrix agent, dressed in a suit and not eating a thing, asks, "Do we have a deal, Mr. Reagan?"

Reagan, looking like a balding motorcycle gang member and eating a juicy steak, says, "I know this steak doesn't exist. I know that when I put it in my mouth, the Matrix is telling my brain that it is juicy and delicious. After nine years, you know what I realize?"—he takes a bite of the steak and sighs—"Ignorance is bliss."

"Then we have a deal?" asks the agent.

"I don't want to remember nothing," says Reagan. "Nothing! You understand? And I want to be rich. You know, someone important—like an actor."

"Whatever you want, Mr. Reagan."

Elapsed time: This scene lasts less than two minutes and starts at about one hour and three minutes into the movie.

Content: Rated R for excessive violence and some language

Citation: *The Matrix* (Warner Brothers, 1999), written and directed by Andy Wachowski and Larry Wachowski

submitted by Bill White, Paramount, California

7. BAPTISM

The Piano

Topic: *Dying to the Past Brings Freedom*

Texts: *Matthew 28:19; Mark 16:16; Romans 6:1–4; Colossians 2:11–12; 1 Peter 3:18–22*

Keywords: *Baptism; Death to Sin; Disabilities; Dying to Self; Forgiveness; Freedom; New Life; Salvation; Shame; Sin; Slavery; Spiritual Bondage*

The Piano chronicles the journey toward emotional freedom of a nineteenth-century single mother named Ada. Motivated by the promise of an arranged marriage, Ada (played by Holly Hunter) moves with her young daughter, Flora, from Scotland to the New Zealand outback. Ada is mute, unable to speak since childhood. She lives in an emotional prison of shame and anger. Flora, conceived out of wedlock, is a reminder of her failures. Ada's sole source of pleasure is her piano, which she brought with her from Scotland.

In New Zealand she marries a Kiwi farmer who turns out to be abusive. A mysterious man by the name of George (Harvey Keitel) arranges to take her away from the abusive marriage, along with her daughter and her cherished piano. They are to escape by sea. As they row from shore toward an awaiting ship, the weight of the piano begins to sink the dinghy. In that moment, Ada suddenly gains insight into her life. She realizes that her piano is a symbol of her shame and regret.

Ada signals to push the piano out of the boat.

"What did she say?" George asks Flora.

"She says, 'throw the piano overboard,'" Flora replies.

Convinced that the piano can be saved, George counters, "It's quite safe. They are managing."

More determined, Flora speaks on her mute mother's behalf. "She says to throw it overboard. She doesn't want it. She says it's spoiled."

Finally George gives in to Ada's request. But as the piano splashes into the sea, a rope tied to the piano encircles Ada's boot. Ada is pulled into the sea and sinks with the piano. She kicks and frees her foot from the boot and then frantically swims back to the surface. When her head breaks the water, she gasps her first breath as a free woman, released from the bondage of shame.

In a similar way, we find freedom in the waters of baptism. When we die to ourselves and to our past, to our passions and sins and possessions, we are set free to live for God.

Elapsed time: Measured from the beginning of the opening credit, this scene begins at 01:49:54 and lasts about three minutes.

Content: Rated R for sexual situations and language

Citation: *The Piano* (Miramax Films, 1993), written and directed by Jane Campion

submitted by Greg Asimakoupoulos, Naperville, Illinois, and Doug Scott, Elgin, Illinois

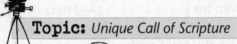

8. BIBLE

The Hurricane

Topic: *Unique Call of Scripture*

Texts: *Isaiah 55:11; 1 Thessalonians 1:5;
1 Thessalonians 2:13; 2 Timothy 3:16;
Hebrews 4:12–13; 1 Peter 1:23*

Keywords: *Authority of Scripture; Bible; Books; Discipleship; Justice; Mentor; Mentoring; Prisons; Race Relations;
Redemption; Relationships; Role Models; Scripture*

In the movie *The Hurricane,* based on real events, Denzel Washington plays boxer Rubin "Hurricane" Carter, a man whose
dreams of winning the title were destroyed when he was arrested
and convicted for the 1966 murders of three people. Carter, serving
three natural life terms, channels his frustration and despair by writing an autobiography from his cell.

Seven years after the book is published, an alienated black youth
named Lesra (played by Vicellous Reon Shannon) is being taught to
read by three white mentors who have taken him into their Toronto
home. One of his three friends takes him to a used book sale, where
he picks up Carter's book. Lesra asks, "How do you know which book
to pick?"

His friend wisely answers, "Sometimes we don't pick the books
we read. They pick us."

Lesra finds purpose and inspiration in Carter's story and begins
writing to Hurricane. A mentoring relationship develops, and eventually Lesra's friends take up Carter's cause and vow to fight for his
release from prison. Carter, at first skeptical of Lesra's white friends,

is eventually won over by their compassionate dedication. He later tells Lesra, "Hate put me in prison. Love's gonna bust me out."

His twenty-year fight for justice ends in triumphant freedom, and he celebrates the victory with his "little brother"—the young man inspired by his book. Toward the end of the movie, while waiting for the judge's ruling, Hurricane asks young Lesra, "What was the first book you ever bought?"

"Yours," he answers.

"Do you think that was an accident?" Hurricane asks.

"No."

At that moment, young Lesra was no doubt thinking back to the words of his mentor: "Sometimes we don't pick the books we read. They pick us."

The Bible is such a book. You can't read it without getting the sense that it picked you, that the Author had you in mind as he wrote.

Elapsed time: Begin at "Universal Pictures and Beacon Pictures Present." Scene 1: Lesra buys the book—00:13:53 to 00:14:34. Scene 2: "Sometimes we don't pick the books we read. They pick us"—00:14:45 to 00:15:16. Scene 3: Hurricane asks Lesra, "What was the first book you ever bought?"—02:12:02 to 02:14:00.

Content: Rated R for some profanity and brief but extreme violence

Citation: *The Hurricane* (Universal Pictures and Beacon Pictures, 1999), written by Armyan Bernstein and Dan Gordon (based on *The Sixteenth Round* by Rubin Carter and *Lazarus and the Hurricane* by Sam Chaiton and Terry Swinton), directed by Norman Jewison

submitted by Clark Cothern, Tecumseh, Michigan

9. BROKENNESS

Star Trek V

Topic: *Man's Need for a Healer*

Texts: *Psalm 23; Psalm 30:2; Matthew 4:23–24;
John 4:13–14; 2 Corinthians 1:3–7;
2 Timothy 1:10; James 5:16*

Keywords: *Brokenness; Burdens; Christ's Love; Comfort;
Compassion; Deliverance; Healing; Pain; Savior; Sorrow;
Suffering*

The movie *Star Trek V: The Final Frontier* begins with a mysterious scene. A human-looking alien named J'onn is toiling beneath a blazing sun. Ragged and malnourished, he drills in vain for water. There are hundreds of holes in the earth around him. Suddenly, he hears the heavy pounding of hoofs. A caped rider on horseback thunders ominously toward him. J'onn releases his drilling device, hurries toward his rifle, and raises his gun toward the fast approaching rider. The rider pulls up short and after a few moments of silence says, "I thought weapons were forbidden on this planet." Powerfully built, the rider swings down from the saddle. He continues, "Besides, I can't believe you'd kill me for a field of empty holes."

Pathetically, J'onn replies, "It's all I have." He seems to sag under the exhausting weight of his burdens.

"Your pain runs deep," the rider says.

Sobbing, J'onn says, "What do you know of my pain?"

"Let us explore it together," the rider says. J'onn begins to tremble, and tears flood down his dirty cheeks. The rider continues,

"Each man hides a secret pain. It must be exposed and reckoned with. It must be dragged from darkness and forced into the light. Share your pain. Share your pain with me, and gain strength from the sharing."

J'onn cries out in anguish, and finally rests his head on the rider's chest. A calmness comes over J'onn, who is baffled but gratefully transformed by the stranger's compassion.

Elapsed time: This scene begins immediately following the opening credit and lasts approximately three minutes.

Content: Rated PG for mild profanity and violence

Citation: *Star Trek V: The Final Frontier* (Paramount, 1989), written by David Loughery (based on a story by William Shatner, David Loughery, and Harve Bennet), directed by William Shatner

*submitted by Jerry De Luca, Montreal West,
Quebec, Canada*

10. CALLING

Dead Poets Society

Topic: *Our "Verse" in Life's Play*

Texts: *Psalm 8:5; Ecclesiastes 3:9–14; John 10:10*

Keywords: *Calling; Image of God; Inspiration of Persons; Meaning of Life; Mission; Purpose; Roles; Wisdom*

The movie *Dead Poets Society* tells the story of a controversial English teacher, John Keating, who shakes up a New England prep school for boys in the 1950s. While at Welton Academy, Keating (played by Robin Williams) introduces his students to classic poets, teaching them to look at life from new vantage points instead of simply relying on knowledge that has been passed down to them.

Inspired by their mentor's example, the boys resurrect a "society of dead poets" that Keating established while he was a student at Welton. Because of the club, a particularly shy student finds the courage to poetically express himself, and another student pursues acting despite his father's disapproval. In the film, Keating represents a Christ figure, inspiring his "disciples" to resist traditionalism and embrace their unique callings.

One day Keating invites his students to tear out the introductory chapter of their textbooks—a chapter that instructs students how to methodically analyze poetry, as though reading poetry were a science. Keating wants his students to *feel* the poetry, not rate it like the latest album on *American Bandstand*. Crouching in the middle of his students, he tells them to huddle up. Like a coach at halftime, he addresses his students: "We don't read and write poetry because it's cute. We read and write poetry because we are members of the human race. And the human race is filled with passion. Medicine, law, business, engineering—these are noble pursuits and necessary to sustain life. But, poetry, beauty, romance, love—these are what we stay alive for."

Mr. Keating then proceeds to quote from a poem by Walt Whitman:

> O me! O life!... of the questions of these recurring;
> Of the endless trains of the faithless—of cities filled with the
>   foolish;
> What good amid these, O me, O life?

The students listen carefully and recognize that the poet is asking a rhetorical question.

Mr. Keating continues:

> Answer: That you are here—that life exists, and identity;
> That the powerful play goes on, and you may contribute a verse.

Keating repeats, "That the powerful play goes on, and you may contribute a verse"—then pauses, looks around at his students, and asks, "And what will your verse be?"

Elapsed time: Measured from the beginning of the opening credit, this scene begins at 00:24:55 and lasts approximately one and one-half minutes.

Content: Rated PG for mild profanity

Citation: *Dead Poets Society* (Touchstone, 1989), written by Tom Schulman, directed by Peter Weir

submitted by Greg Asimakoupoulos, Naperville, Illinois

11. CARING

Patch Adams

Topic: *Christlike Caring*

Texts: *Isaiah 1:10–18; Luke 18:15; John 4:27; John 10:3; 1 John 3:18*

Keywords: *Caring; Christian Life; Christlikeness; Community; Evangelism; Love; Relationships*

Patch Adams is a movie based on the true story of a medical student who discovers the healing qualities of humor while treating patients. Hunter "Patch" Adams (played by comedian Robin Williams) is frustrated by school policies that encourage an impersonal approach to practicing medicine.

Borrowing a white lab coat, Patch disguises himself in a group of third-year students making rounds. The teaching physician impersonally describes the symptoms and diagnoses of each patient.

As the teacher approaches a young woman with open sores on her feet and legs, he says, "Here we have a juvenile onset diabetic with poor circulation and diabetic ulcers with lymphedema and evidence of gangrene. Questions?"

A student asks, "Any osteomyelitis?"

"None apparent, although not definitive."

Another student inquires as to the appropriate treatment.

"To stabilize the blood sugar. Consider antibiotics and perhaps amputation," he answers.

The patient cringes when she hears the frightening words offered by a doctor who has not yet even acknowledged her presence. From the back of the room, Patch's voice is heard.

"What's her name? I was just wondering the patient's name."

Caught off guard, the physician struggles to find a name on the chart before announcing, "Margery."

As the class moves out of the room toward the next patient, Patch lingers at the bedside of this woman and reaches out to touch her shoulder as he calls her by name.

Elapsed time: Measured from the beginning of the opening credit, this scene begins at 00:24:50 and lasts approximately six minutes.

Content: Rated PG-13 for profanity, vulgarity, and some violence

Citation: *Patch Adams* (Universal Studios, 1998), written by Patch Adams and Steve Oedekerk, directed by Tom Shadyac

submitted by Greg Asimakoupoulos, Naperville, Illinois

12. CHALLENGES

Hoosiers

Topic: *Facing New Challenges with Faith*

Texts: *Exodus 14:29–17:16; Deuteronomy 31:3–8;
1 Samuel 17:33–37; Matthew 28:19–20;
2 Corinthians 1:10; Philippians 4:13*

Keywords: *Challenges; Dependence on God; Evangelism;
Faith; Fear; Great Commission; Help from God; Ministry;
Overcoming; Trials; Trust*

Hoosiers is the Cinderella story of a small-town Indiana high school basketball team that overcomes adversity in order to win the state championship. Gene Hackman plays the part of Norman Dale, a former college coach with a maligned past, who is hired to coach the boy's team from Hickory, Indiana.

When the team arrives at Butler Field House in Indianapolis to play for the state championship, the players' jaws drop at the size of the six-thousand-seat arena with its freestanding hoops and suspended scoreboard.

Coach Dale senses that they are intimidated. He instructs one of his players to take a tape measure and mark off the distance from the basket to the free throw line.

"What's the distance?" the coach inquires.

"Fifteen feet," the player with the tape calls out.

Coach Dale tells the team's shortest player to climb up on the shoulders of the tallest player and measure the height of the basket.

"How high is it?" he asks.

The boy says, "Ten feet."

The coach says, "I believe you'll find these are the exact same measurements as our gym back in Hickory."

The team laughs, and the tension eases. They move on to prepare for the game.

When we face new challenges and trials, we can be confident that, just as God helped us in the past, he will also help us in the future.

Elapsed time: Measured from the beginning of the opening credit, this scene begins at 01:29:35 and lasts about five and one-half minutes.

Content: Rated PG

Citation: *Hoosiers* (Hemdale Film Corporation, 1986), written by Angelo Pizzo, directed by David Anspaugh

submitted by Greg Asimakoupoulos, Naperville, Illinois, and Doug Scott, Elgin, Illinois

13. CHRIST, SUBSTITUTE FOR HUMANITY

Beauty and the Beast

Topic: Sacrificial Love

Texts: John 3:16; John 15:13; Galatians 1:4; Hebrews 10:14

Keywords: Christ the Burden Bearer; Christ the Only Savior; Christ the Substitute for Humanity; Christ's Love; Freedom; Love; Sacrifice; Salvation; Self-Sacrifice

Beauty and the Beast, a Walt Disney animated movie, tells the story of a beautiful French girl named Belle, who finds the love of Beast, a prince condemned long ago to live a life of shame and ugliness because he could not love.

One night, Belle's father, Maurice, gets lost in a forest and is thrown from his horse. When the horse returns without Maurice the next day, Belle sets off to find him. She follows her father's horse to an imposing castle set deep within the forest. The castle looms over Belle, its twisted, hulking form inspiring fear. When she finds her father's hat lying inside the gate, she cautiously enters despite her fright.

Once inside, a talking candlestick leads Belle to a dungeon, where she finds her father huddled in a cell—alone, cold, and sick. Maurice, having seen the monstrous beast who put him there, pleads with Belle to leave. Belle refuses and tries to free him.

Suddenly a booming voice growls from the darkness. "What are you doing here?" Beast challenges Belle from the shadows.

Belle learns that her father is being held for trespassing and that there is no escape from the punishment for his offense. As her father gasps and wheezes, Belle offers, "Take me instead!"

Beast is momentarily startled and asks, "You would take his place?"

"If I did, would you let him go?" Belle bargains.

"Yes, but you must promise to stay here forever," answers Beast.

"You have my word," Belle vows.

"Done!"

Though puzzled by her sacrifice, Beast makes the trade and frees Belle's father.

Elapsed time: Measured from the beginning of the opening credit, Belle begins her search for Maurice at 00:22:00, and the scene ends at 00:24:00 with the sacrificial substitution.

Content: Rated G

Citation: *Beauty and the Beast* (Disney, 1991), written by Roger Allers and Linda Woolverton, directed by Gary Trousdale and Kirk Wise

submitted by Jennifer Tatum, Romeoville, Illinois

14. CHRIST, SUBSTITUTE FOR HUMANITY

The Lion King

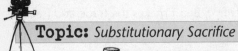

Topic: *Substitutionary Sacrifice*

Texts: *Isaiah 9:6; John 3:16; John 15:13; Romans 5:8; 2 Corinthians 5:15; 1 Thessalonians 5:10; 1 John 4:9–10*

Keywords: *Atonement; Christ the Substitute for Humanity; Cross; Death; Devotion; Evil; Loyalty; Redemption; Sacrifice*

Disney's animated film *The Lion King* portrays the primal struggle between good and evil through its main character. Simba, a cub on his way to becoming the lion king, faces trials that help him understand his purpose in life.

From the time of Simba's birth, Scar (Simba's uncle) has resented that he has been replaced as next in line to the throne. He knows the crown prince is entitled to the kingdom's wealth and power. Determined to become king, Scar hatches a deadly plot. He entices Simba to a rock in a clearing, where he signals the hyenas—his evil accomplices—to begin a stampede of wildebeests. He knows that as soon as Mufasa, Simba's father, hears that Simba is in trouble, Mufasa will come to rescue his son. Both will then be caught in his deadly trap.

The earth trembles as the stampeding animals approach the innocent cub. Simba realizes that he is in danger and attempts to outrun the stampede. Just in the nick of time, his father, Mufasa, arrives, and with a flick of his paw he pushes young Simba to safety. But in the process the king is trampled. A bleeding Mufasa tries to scale a steep cliff, where his brother watches with glee. Instead of reaching out to pull his brother up, Scar claws the king's paws, causing Mufasa to fall to his death below.

Young Simba approaches the carcass, unaware that his dad gave his life to save his. He nuzzles his dad's mane and calls out, "Dad. Dad. Get up, Dad."

Elapsed time: Measured from the beginning of the opening credit, this scene begins at 00:32:10 and lasts approximately five minutes.

Content: Rated G

Citation: *The Lion King* (Disney, 1994), written by Jim Capobianco, Irene Mecchi, Jonathan Roberts, and Linda Woolverton, directed by Roger Allers and Rob Minkoff

submitted by Greg Asimakoupoulos, Naperville, Illinois

15. COMMUNITY

I Am Sam

Topic: *Friends Help Raise Daughter*

Texts: *Proverbs 17:17; Ecclesiastes 4:9–12; Acts 2:44; Acts 4:32; 2 Corinthians 8:1–5; 1 John 3:16–18*

Keywords: *Brotherly Love; Child Rearing; Church; Community; Friendship; Generosity; Giving; Human Help; Love; Money; Parenting; Sharing; Support*

I Am Sam is the story of Sam, an adult with mental disabilities, raising his daughter, Lucy, on his own.

Sam works at Starbucks and hangs out with four other men who also have mental disabilities. Sam's friends are excited about the new addition to Sam's life, often offering to hold or feed little Lucy.

Prior to beginning first grade, Lucy needs new shoes. Money is tight for Sam and his friends. They must walk everywhere they go. Their clothes are simple, if not a little threadbare. Sam's wages at the local Starbucks are barely sufficient for the one-bedroom apartment he and Lucy share. But he and his four faithful friends set out with Lucy to buy her a pair of shoes.

They all take the task seriously as they search for the perfect pair, presenting each offering to Lucy. They find shoes with blinking lights, pink shoes, and leopard-skin shoes five sizes too big. The shoe salesman is somewhat frustrated by this exasperating process, but he cooperates.

When at last they find the perfect pair, Sam asks the shoe salesman the price, and the salesman says, "$16.19 with tax."

The mood becomes uncomfortable as Sam counts out too little money. Sam says, "I only have $6.25." There are people in line behind them, and Lucy begins to exchange nervous glances with Sam and his friends.

"That's all you have?" asks the salesman.

"Yeah," responds Sam, "because I didn't get my whole check, because I had to go to the parent and teacher meeting this week."

"I'm sorry, sir, the price is $16.19."

Sam's friends, without being asked, reach into their pockets to make up the difference. In an instant, all the money that is needed is on the counter. Lucy smiles, and they all leave with balloons.

Elapsed time: Measured from the New Line logo, this scene begins at 00:15:15 and ends at 00:17:24.

Content: Rated PG-13 for language

Citation: *I Am Sam* (New Line Cinema, 2001), written by Jessie Nelson and Kristine Johnson, directed by Jessie Nelson

submitted by David Slagle, Lawrenceville, Georgia

16. COMMUNITY

With Honors

Topic: *Caring Community Becomes Family*

Texts: *Psalm 68:6; Proverbs 17:17; Ecclesiastes 4:9–12; John 13:35; Acts 2:42–47; Acts 4:32–35; Romans 12:10; Ephesians 2:19–22*

Keywords: *Caring; Church; Church as the Family of God; Community; Compassion; Family; Friendship; Homelessness; Love; Relationships*

In the 1994 movie *With Honors,* Joe Pesci plays the role of Simon Wilder, a homeless vagrant living in the boiler room of the Harvard University library. His life has been marked by a series of bad choices and bad breaks. Attempting to make the best of his circumstances, Simon has secretly created a cozy, book-lined living space undetected by the university's security team.

One day Simon finds the one and only copy of a senior's thesis. It belongs to Harvard student Monty Kessler (played by Brendan Fraser). When the panicked student discovers the whereabouts of his term project, he offers Simon food and shelter in exchange for the term paper. Rather than giving up the thesis all at once, an intelligent Simon offers one page of it per each act of kindness. A beautiful friendship emerges between this unlikely pair.

When it becomes clear that Simon is dying from a lung disease caused by excessive exposure to asbestos, Monty and his three housemates care for him as though they were his family. Even though Monty's care for this homeless man will prevent him from getting his thesis in on time (thus forfeiting his right to graduate "with honors"), he willingly demonstrates compassion.

When Simon eventually dies, his surrogate family grieves deeply. The foursome gathers in the cemetery to pay their last respects to Simon before his casket is lowered into the ground. Monty pulls out a sheet of paper from his coat.

"Simon wrote this and asked me to read it:

"Simon B. Wilder bit it on Wednesday. He saw the world out of the porthole of a leaky freighter. He was a collector of memories and interrupted a lecture at Harvard. In fifty years on earth he did only one thing that he regretted. He is survived by his 'family': Jeff Hawks, who always remembers to flush; Everett Calloway, who knows how to use words; Courtney Blumenthal, who is strong and also knows how to love; and Montgomery Kessler, who will graduate from life with honors and no regrets."

Elapsed time: Measured from the beginning of the opening credit, this scene begins at 01:30:10 and lasts about three and one-half minutes.

Content: Rated PG-13 for mild profanity and sensuality

Citation: *With Honors* (Warner Brothers, 1994), written by William Mastrosimone, directed by Alek Keshishian

submitted by Greg Asimakoupoulos, Naperville, Illinois

17. COMPLACENCY

Dead Poets Society

Topic: *Seize the Day*

Texts: *1 Corinthians 15:58; Hebrews 11; Hebrews 12:1–3; Revelation 7:9–17*

Keywords: *Complacency; Diligence; Ministry; Service; Spiritual Gifts*

The movie *Dead Poets Society* is about a controversial English teacher, John Keating, who shakes up a New England prep school for boys in the 1950s. While at Welton Academy, Keating (played by Robin Williams) introduces his students to classic poets, teaching them to look at life from new vantage points instead of simply relying on knowledge that has been passed down to them.

Inspired by their mentor's example, the boys resurrect a society of dead poets that Keating established while he was a student at Welton. Because of the club, a particularly shy student finds the courage to express himself poetically, and another student begins acting despite his father's disapproval.

On the first day of school, Mr. Keating walks into his class whistling Tchaikovsky's "1812 Overture." At once, the students recognize that he is unlike any other teacher they've had at Welton Academy. He motions for them to follow him out into the hall, where they stand in front of the school's trophy case. A student reads aloud a famous poem about the passage of time, which Keating proceeds to interpret.

Keating says, "We are food for worms, lads. Believe it or not, each and every one of us in this room is one day going to stop breathing, turn cold, and die." Motioning them to draw nearer to the display of aged photographs, he continues. "I'd like you to step forward over here and peruse some of the faces from the past. You've walked past them many times, but I don't really think you've ever looked at them. They are not that different from you, are they? Same haircuts, full of hormones, just like you. Invincible, just like you feel. The world is their oyster. They believe they're destined for great things. Their eyes are full of hope, just like you. Did they wait till it was too late to make from their lives even one iota of what they were capable? Because you see, gentlemen, these boys are now fertilizing daffodils. If you listen real close, you can hear them whispering their legacy to you. Go on, lean in. Listen. Do you hear it?"

As the boys press their noses near the trophy case, Mr. Keating stands behind them and whispers, "Carpe diem. Seize the day!"

Elapsed time: Measured from the beginning of the opening credit, this scene begins at 00:11:33 and lasts approximately five minutes.

Content: Rated PG for mild profanity

Citation: *Dead Poets Society* (Touchstone Pictures, 1989), written by Tom Schulman, directed by Peter Weir

submitted by Greg Asimakoupoulos, Naperville, Illinois

18. CONFESSION

Dead Man Walking

Topic: *Finding Real Love*

Texts: *Psalm 118:5; Luke 23:40–43; John 8:36;
Romans 3:22–28; 2 Corinthians 5:17;
1 Timothy 1:15–16; James 5:16*

Keywords: *Confession; Conversion; Crime; Death;
Forgiveness; Grace; Love; Mercy; Prisons; Regret; Repentance; Salvation; Sin; Sorrow; Spiritual Death*

The movie *Dead Man Walking* is based on Sister Helen Prejean's mission to care for the soul of death row inmate Matthew Poncelet. Poncelet (played by Sean Penn) awaits execution for brutally killing a young man and woman. Throughout the movie Poncelet vehemently denies any wrongdoing, even though the evidence contradicts him. At one point, Sister Helen (played by Susan Sarandon) gives him a Bible and tells him to read the Gospel of John. She persistently tries to help him face the truth, but he resists, blaming anyone else he can think of.

One emotional scene—the climax of the movie—shows Poncelet finally admitting his guilt. Poncelet recalls, "My mama kept saying, 'It wasn't you, Matt. It wasn't you.'"

"Your mama loves you, Matt," responds Sister Helen.

Grieved by guilt, Poncelet begins to confess, but lapses as tears flood his eyes. As Sister Helen probes him further, Poncelet admits, "I killed [the boy]." Sister Helen then asks about Hope, the raped and murdered girl. Again, Poncelet forthrightly confesses.

"Do you take responsibility for both of their deaths?" asks Sister Helen.

Poncelet responds, "Yes, ma'am. . . . When the lights dim at night, I kneel down by my bunk and pray for those kids. . . . I've never done that before."

Sister Helen comforts Poncelet, saying, "There is a place of sorrow only God can touch. You did a terrible thing, Matt, a terrible thing. But you have a dignity now. Nobody can take that away from you. . . . You are a son of God, Matthew Poncelet."

Sobbing deeply, Poncelet says, "Nobody ever called me no son of God before. They called me a son-of-you-know-what lots of times, but never no son of God. . . . I just hope my death can give those parents some relief. I really do."

"Well," continues Sister Helen, "maybe the best thing you can give to the Percys and the Delacroixs is a wish for their peace."

Poncelet says, "I never had no real love myself. I never loved a woman or anybody else. . . . It about figures I would have to die to find love. . . . Thank you for loving me."

Elapsed time: Measured from the beginning of the opening credit, this scene begins at 01:34:39 and ends at 01:37:25. Note: Before showing the clip it may be helpful to mention that the conversation can be difficult to understand at points.

Content: Rated R for depiction of rape and murder as well as for profanity and mature themes

Citation: *Dead Man Walking* (Polygram Filmed Entertainment, 1995), written and directed by Tim Robbins (based on the nonfiction book by Sister Helen Prejean)

submitted by Bill White, Paramount, California

19. CONSCIENCE

Roman Holiday

Topic: *A Guilty Conscience*

Texts: *Psalm 51:3–10; Proverbs 28:1*

Keywords: *Conscience; Deceit; Deception; Guilt; Lying*

Roman Holiday is the classic 1953 movie about a frustrated princess who escapes from her royal entourage while on a trip to Rome. While incognito, she falls in love with an American newspaperman. The princess, played by Audrey Hepburn, is weary of the pomp and circumstance of the royal life and longs to do the things that common folk enjoy. Joe Bradley, the American newspaperman (played by Gregory Peck), recognizes the disguised princess and sees an opportunity for a big story. Bradley hides his own identity as a journalist so that he can escort the princess around the tourist sites of Rome and scoop a great news story.

Both Bradley and the princess lie to each other. In one suspenseful scene, Bradley takes the princess to The Mouth of Truth, an ancient relief of a round monstrous face with menacing eyes and a hole in the wall for a mouth. The legend behind the relief is as terrifying as the face. Bradley, who knows the princess is lying, tells the princess the legend.

"Legend has it," he says, "that if you stick your hand in the mouth and give it a lie, it will bite your hand off." The princess looks horrified as she grapples with her deceit. "Give it a try," Bradley urges.

Not wanting to reveal her deceit, the princess tentatively moves her hand toward the mouth. Just before putting her hand in The

Mouth of Truth, she backs away and says, "You do it!" Her guilty conscience causes her to fall victim to a silly superstition.

The drama continues as Bradley slowly puts his hand in The Mouth of Truth. As his arm fills up the hole, the mouth appears poised to bite. Bradley offers a calm smile to the princess. Then he cries out, acting as though The Mouth of Truth has clamped down on his hand. He is, of course, joking, but the princess falls for it completely.

Elapsed time: Measured from the beginning of the opening credit, the scene begins at 01:18:13 and ends at 01:19:38.

Content: Not rated

Citation: *Roman Holiday* (Universal, 1953), written by Dalton Trumbo, Ian McLellan Hunter, and John Dighton, directed by William Wyler

submitted by David Slagle, Lawrenceville, Georgia

20. CONSEQUENCES

Groundhog Day

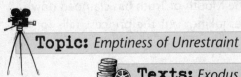

Topic: *Emptiness of Unrestraint*

Texts: *Exodus 20:1–17; Numbers 32:23; Proverbs 14:12; Ecclesiastes 2:10–11; Galatians 6:7–9*

Keywords: *Accountability; Commandments; Consequences; Judgment; Morality; Selfishness; Self-Sufficiency; Sin; Sowing and Reaping; Ten Commandments*

Groundhog Day exposes the emptiness of a life without moral accountability. In this insightful comedy, an egocentric TV weatherman named Phil (played by Bill Murray) is assigned to cover the festivities of Groundhog Day in Punxsutawney, Pennsylvania. Due to an unexpected snowstorm, Phil must spend an extra night in this little town with his producer and love interest, Rita (played by Andie MacDowell).

When Phil awakens the next morning, he discovers it is still February 2. He realizes he is stuck in a twenty-four-hour loop of Groundhog Days. No matter what he does, he wakes up every morning as though nothing had happened the day before.

With newfound friends, Phil contemplates what life would be like if there were no consequences. There would be no hangovers. People could do whatever they wanted. Before the night is over, Phil ends up being chased by police, drives into a mailbox, hits a parked car, and is arrested. But when Phil wakes up, it is Groundhog Day once again.

On this particular day Phil goes out to lunch with Rita. He orders most everything on the menu and lights up a cigarette.

Curious about his strange behavior, Rita asks, "Don't you worry about cholesterol, lung cancer, love handles?"

"I don't worry about anything anymore," Phil responds.

"What makes you so special?" Rita counters. "Everybody worries about something."

Phil contends that his lack of concern over any consequences (including the wages of not flossing) is what makes him special.

Rita responds by quoting a poem by Sir Walter Scott:

> *The wretch, concentrated all in self,*
> *Living, shall forfeit fair renown,*
> *And, doubly dying, shall go down*
> *To the vile dust from whence he sprung*
> *Unwept, unhonour'd, and unsung.*

Phil attempts to shrug off her wise commentary as irrelevant, but it is obvious that a world not governed by moral accountability is an empty one indeed.

Elapsed time: Measured from the beginning of the opening credit, this scene begins at 00:31:48 and lasts about five and one-half minutes.

Content: Rated PG for language

Citation: *Groundhog Day* (Columbia Pictures, 1993), written and directed by Harold Ramis

submitted by Greg Asimakoupoulos, Naperville, Illinois, and Doug Scott, Elgin, Illinois

21. CONVICTIONS

Chariots of Fire

Topic: *Living by Principle*

Texts: *Isaiah 40:28–31; Acts 20:24; 1 Corinthians 9:24–27*

Keywords: *Convictions; Devotion; Losing; Meaning of Life; Principles; Purpose; Sabbath; Sacrifice; Surrender; Winning*

The film *Chariots of Fire* is a true story about two British runners competing in the 1924 Olympics. Eric Liddell, a devout Christian, was encouraged by his missionary dad to "run in God's Name, and let the world stand back and wonder." Contrarily, Liddell's teammate Harold Abrahams (played by Ben Cross) ran for personal glory.

On the boat to the Paris Olympics, Liddell (played by Ian Charleson) learned that, in order to compete in the 100-meter dash—his best distance and the race he was favored to win—he had to run the qualifying heats on Sunday. He resolved not to run on the Sabbath. During a reception in Paris, Liddell was pressured by Scotland's aristocracy to run.

Lord Birkenhead began: "We decided to invite you for a little chat to see if there is any way we can help resolve this situation."

Lord Cadogan then added, "There's only one way to resolve this situation. That's for this man [Liddell] to change his mind."

Unruffled by the pressure, Liddell responded, "I'm afraid there are no ways, sir. I won't run on the Sabbath, and that's final. God made countries, and God makes the kings and the rules by which they govern. And those rules say that the Sabbath is his, and I, for one, intend to keep it that way."

The Sunday Eric Liddell could have been running, he worshiped in a Paris church and preached from Isaiah 40—"But they that wait upon the LORD shall renew their strength; they shall mount up with wings as eagles; they shall run, and not be weary; and they shall walk, and not faint."

Harold Abrahams, however, prepared for the race and confessed to Liddell, "I used to be afraid to lose. But now I am afraid to win. I have ten seconds in which to prove the reason for my existence, and even then, I'm not sure I will." Abrahams did win the gold medal in the 100-meter, while Liddell applauded him on the sidelines. But his gold medal gave him only fleeting satisfaction.

Later in the Olympics, Liddell competed in the 400-meter, an event he had not trained for and was not favored to win. Surprisingly, Liddell not only won but broke the world record in the process.

In 1925, Eric Liddell went to China to serve as a teacher and missionary. When life in China became so dangerous that the British government advised British nationals to leave, Liddell stayed behind and was interned in a prison camp, where he died of a brain tumor in 1945. His last words are reported to have been, "It's complete surrender."

Elapsed time: Measured from the beginning of the opening credit, the scene with the Scottish aristocracy begins at 01:25:35 and lasts approximately seven minutes.

Content: Rated PG for mild profanity

Citation: *Chariots of Fire* (Warner Brothers, 1981), written by Colin Welland, directed by Hugh Hudson

submitted by Aaron Goerner, New Hartford, New York

22. CONVICTIONS

The Remains of the Day

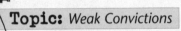

Topic: *Weak Convictions*

Texts: *Joshua 24:14–15; Ecclesiastes 5:4–7; Isaiah 1:11–17; Matthew 13:20–21; Matthew 21:28–32; Matthew 25:34–45*

Keywords: *Bigotry; Choices; Commitment; Compromise; Convictions; Cowardice; Fear; Hypocrisy; Racism; Social Action*

The *Remains of the Day* explores the repressed love between the devoted English butler Mr. Stevens (Anthony Hopkins) and the head housekeeper Miss Kenton (Emma Thompson) in 1930s England. The master of the house, Lord Darlington (James Fox), is being influenced by the Nazis to establish rapport between themselves and the British government. Nazi representatives are periodic guests in his house.

Lord Darlington addresses Mr. Stevens: "Stevens, we have some refugee girls on staff at the moment, I believe."

"We do, my Lord. Two housemaids. Elsa and Emma."

"You'll have to let them go, I'm afraid."

"Let them go, my Lord?"

"It's regrettable, Stevens, but we have no choice. You've got to see the whole thing in context. I have the well-being of my guests to consider."

"My Lord, may I say, they work extremely well. They're intelligent, polite, and very clean."

"I'm sorry, Stevens, but I've looked into the matter very carefully. There are larger issues at stake. I'm sorry, but there it is. They're Jews."

In the next scene, Stevens and Miss Kenton are having tea together in one of the servants' quarters.

Miss Kenton is flustered and upset. "You're saying that Elsa and Emma are to be dismissed because they're Jewish?"

Stevens answers firmly and calmly, "His Lordship has made his decision. There is nothing for you and I to discuss."

Miss Kenton says, "You realize if these girls have no work they could be sent back to Germany!"

"It is out of our hands."

"I'm telling you, Mr. Stevens, if you dismiss these girls it will be wrong. A sin. As any sin if ever was one."

"Miss Kenton, there are many things you and I don't understand in the world of today—whereas his Lordship understands fully and has studied the larger issues at stake concerning, say, the nature of Jewry."

"Mr. Stevens, I warn you. If these girls go, I shall leave this home."

In the third scene, Stevens and Miss Kenton have just finished an interview of a candidate for one of the now vacant positions.

Stevens says to Miss Kenton, "Didn't you say you were leaving because of the German girls?"

Miss Kenton appears remorseful. "I'm not leaving. I've nowhere to go. I have no family. I'm a coward. I'm frightened of leaving and that's the truth. All I see in the world is limits, and it frightens me. That's all my high principles are worth, Mr. Stevens. I'm ashamed of myself."

Elapsed time: Measured from the opening credits, the scenes begin at 01:07:40 and end at 01:11:40.

Content: Rated PG for mature themes

Citation: *The Remains of the Day* (Columbia Pictures, 1993), written by Ruth Prawer Jhabvala (based on the novel by Kazuo Ishiguro), directed by James Ivory

submitted by Jerry De Luca, Montreal West,
Quebec, Canada

23. COURAGE

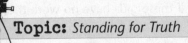

Dead Poets Society

Topic: *Standing for Truth*

Texts: *Matthew 10:22; John 15:18–27*

Keywords: *Courage; Devotion; Faithfulness; Loyalty; Persecution*

The movie *Dead Poets Society* is about a controversial teacher and a class of teenage boys at a prestigious New England prep school in the 1950s. John Keating (played by Robin Williams) challenges the status quo at an institution where traditions have calcified. Keating, who attended Welton Academy a decade earlier, introduces his young disciples to a thirst for knowledge and life by exposing them to the classical poets. He teaches them to look at life from new vantage points.

To illustrate his approach, he once had them stand on his desk to gain new perspective on the classroom they've only seen from their seats. Inspired by their mentor's example, the boys resurrect the "Dead Poets Society" he established at the school while he was a student.

The film portrays Keating as a Jesus figure, inspiring his disciples to swim against the tide of dead traditionalism. Finding precedence in Walt Whitman's famous poem about Lincoln, Keating invites his students to refer to him as "O Captain, my captain."

But then one of Welton's students commits suicide. The administration blames the suicide on Mr. Keating's unorthodox teaching and dismisses the popular teacher. The headmaster, Mr. Nolan (played by Norman Lloyd), then takes over Mr. Keating's class and reverts to the traditional lecture format.

It is obvious that most of the class is not only grieving the death of their classmate but also the loss of their favorite teacher. A heavy cloud hangs over the class because the administration forced the students to sign a document (under threat of expulsion) implicating Mr. Keating in the student's suicide. The headmaster asks one of the students to read from a certain page in the textbook, only to discover that Mr. Keating had instructed the boys to tear out that section of the book. At this moment, Mr. Keating enters the classroom to retrieve his personal belongings.

As the beloved teacher self-consciously walks past a student, the young man blurts out, "Mr. Keating, they made everybody sign. You've got to believe me. It's true!"

Keating smiles and says, "I do believe you, Todd."

Meanwhile, Mr. Nolan, incensed by the interruption, insists that Mr. Keating leave the room.

"But it wasn't his fault," Todd contends, gaining courage by the moment.

"One more outburst from you or anybody else, and you're out of this school," Mr. Nolan threatens. "Leave, Mr. Keating. I said leave."

At that moment, Todd stands up on his desk and calls out, "O Captain, my captain." While Mr. Nolan shouts his disapproval and continues his threats, student after student risks the consequences by standing on their desks and pledging their allegiance to someone who had awakened life within them.

Elapsed time: Measured from the beginning of the opening credit, the scene begins at 02:00:00 and lasts nearly five minutes.

Content: Rated PG for mild profanity

Citation: *Dead Poets Society* (Touchstone, 1989), written by Tom Schulman, directed by Peter Weir

submitted by Greg Asimakoupoulos, Naperville, Illinois

24. DEDICATION

The Patriot

Topic: *Perseverance despite Heartbreak*

Texts: *1 Corinthians 11:1; 1 Corinthians 15:58; Galatians 6:9; Philippians 1; Philippians 3:12–17; Colossians 4:17; 1 Timothy 4:11–16; 1 Timothy 6:12; Titus 2:7; Hebrews 10:36*

Keywords: *Commitment; Courage; Death; Dedication; Devotion; Example; Influence; Leadership; Loss; Perseverance; Purpose; Quitting; Sacrifice; Strength*

The 2000 movie *The Patriot* starred Mel Gibson as Benjamin Martin, a reluctant Revolutionary War hero. Martin has an eighteen-year-old son named Gabriel (played by Heath Ledger), who is eager to join the conflict. Gabriel's sentiments for his country are revealed by one pastime: throughout the first half of the movie, Gabriel diligently repairs an American flag he found in the dirt.

Tragically, Gabriel becomes a casualty of the war, and, suffering deep loss, his father Benjamin Martin appears ready to quit the cause. While Martin is grieving at the side of his dead son, Colonel Harry Burwell (Chris Cooper), a Continental officer, attempts to persuade Martin not to quit. He recognizes that Martin has great influence with the soldiers and that his departure would demoralize the troops.

As the scene opens, the colonel says, "Stay the course, Martin. Stay the course."

Grief-stricken, Martin responds, "I've run the course." Resigned to the outcome, the colonel informs the troops, and they ride on, leaving Martin behind.

As Martin loads his son's personal effects on his horse, though, he finds the American flag Gabriel had successfully restored.

As the dejected soldiers ride away, certain they have seen the last of Benjamin Martin, Martin appears in the distance, carrying the flag. With determination in his posture, he rides upright in his saddle, face like flint, the Stars and Stripes whipping in the wind. Martin has been a symbol of perseverance for the men, and there is a triumphant shout of both relief and excitement from the once-weary troops as they see the patriot crest the hill.

Whether leaders at home, school, work, or church, we must never underestimate the power of our influence to demoralize or to rally others. People are watching. Soldiers look to officers. Children look to parents. We must stay the course.

Elapsed time: The scene begins at 02:13:09 and ends at 02:15:50.

Content: Rated R for graphic violence (there is no nudity)

Citation: *The Patriot* (Columbia Pictures, Centropolis Entertainment, 2000), written by Robert Rodat, directed by Roland Emmerich

submitted by David Slagle, Lawrenceville, Georgia

25. DEPENDENCE ON GOD

The Inn of the Sixth Happiness

Topic: *Faith against All Odds*

Texts: *Matthew 14:25–32; Acts 1:8; Acts 20:24; 2 Corinthians 1:8–10; 2 Corinthians 12:9–10; Hebrews 10:35–39; James 1:2–4; 1 Peter 3:13–22*

Keywords: *Adversity; Boldness; Challenges; Courage; Dependence on God; Evangelism; Faith; Faithfulness; Ministry; Missionary; Missions; Obedience; Perseverance; Trust*

The 1958 film *The Inn of the Sixth Happiness* is the true story of Gladys Aylward (played by Ingrid Bergman), an English servant who became a faithful missionary in a remote region of northern China. The China Inland Mission Center in England refused to sponsor her, due to her lack of vocation and experience. Consequently, in 1932 she set out on her own, believing with all her heart that she was called by God. Not officially under the authority of the Mission Center, she was free to stay in China according to her own discretion.

She finds work running an inn for traveling mule drivers. After the death of the inn manager (a seasoned missionary), a government official delivers a letter to Gladys, stating that funding for the inn will be cut off because of her lack of experience.

Bewildered by the news, Gladys expresses her concerns to the Chinese government official who had delivered the message—Captain Lin Nan (played by Curt Jurgens): "One reason and always the same one: I'm not qualified. I was a servant in England. That's what they mean. But I came here when they said I couldn't. And I'll stay here, though they say I can't."

When Captain Lin Nan kindly offers to escort her to Bien Chen, where she will deport, Gladys stubbornly insists, "I'm not going to leave!"

Captain Lin Nan tries to dissuade her—she's broke, and vendors won't give her credit; she has no friends; and she is in an isolated country with inveterate problems. "It isn't your country. It isn't your problem," he says. "You're white. You shouldn't be in China at all."

Emphasizing her resolve to stay, Gladys reminds the captain, "I came here to be of value."

Mildly irritated, the captain says, "How? By trying to make people believe what you believe? By saving souls who don't want to be saved—who will agree to anything for an extra bowl of rice, and laugh at you once the rice is eaten?" When Gladys attempts a retort, he says, "The dangers that confront you—those are real. Leave now, while you still can. Go back to England where you belong."

"If I feel that God wants me in China," Gladys argues, "then that's where I belong."

Lin Nan gives up, leaving Gladys in God's hands. As he leaves, Gladys cries out, "Oh, Captain Lin Nan. I know you think I'm stubborn. But I'm not ungrateful. For you to be concerned, to bother—it is very kind."

"If I were really kind," Lin Nan responds, "I'd have you ordered out of Bien Chen. But since I'm not obsessed with souls or lives, I wish you well."

Because she perseveres, God uses Gladys to convert the village's mandarin governor to Christianity. And when the Japanese army attacks China, she heroically leads over a hundred orphan children to safety through numerous mountains, avoiding enemy soldiers.

Elapsed time: Measured from the beginning of the opening credit, this scene begins at 00:49:00 and ends at 00:52:30.

Content: Not rated

Citation: *The Inn of the Sixth Happiness* (20th Century Fox, 1958), written by Isobel Lennart (based on *The Small Woman* by Alan Burgess), directed by Mark Robson

submitted by Jerry De Luca, Montreal West, Quebec, Canada

26. DETERMINATION

Remember the Titans

Topic: *Willingness to Endure Hardship*

Texts: *Luke 8:15; Luke 21:12–19; Romans 5:3–4; Romans 8:17–18; 1 Corinthians 4:12; 2 Corinthians 1:6; 2 Corinthians 6:4; Philippians 1:29; Colossians 1:11; 2 Timothy 2:3; 2 Timothy 4:5; James 1:2–4*

Keywords: *Determination; Endurance; Hardship; Pain; Perseverance; Strength; Suffering*

Remember the Titans, a movie based on the true story of a 1971 Alexandria, Virginia, football team, offers a message of racial reconciliation. Early in the movie, Coach Herman Boone (played by Denzel Washington) takes his race-divided high school team to a two-week football camp. He works the boys hard, both emotionally and physically, trying desperately to build a sense of team. By the last practice, the boys begin to come together.

During this practice, the football team, outfitted in full pads and white practice uniforms, line up row by row. They vigorously run in place, focused on their conditioning.

Coach Boone yells, "What are you?"

The team shouts back, "Mobile! Agile! Hostile!"

Boone shouts, "And what is pain?"

"French bread!" the young men reply.

Boone hollers, "What is fatigue?"

They bellow, "Army clothes!"

With all his might, Coach Boone yells, "Will—you—ever—quit?"
The Titans roar, "No, we want some mo'! We want some mo'!
We want some mo'!"

Elapsed time: Measured from the beginning of the
opening credit, this scene begins at 00:49:52 and
ends at 00:50:11.

Content: Rated PG for thematic elements and mild
profanity

Citation: *Remember the Titans* (Disney, 2000), written
by Gregory Allen Howard, directed by Boaz Yakin

submitted by Lee Eclov, Lake Forest, Illinois

27. DISCIPLINE

Shrek

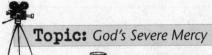

Topic: *God's Severe Mercy*

Texts: *Deuteronomy 31:6; Isaiah 43:1–3; Jeremiah 29:11; Romans 8:28; Hebrews 12:5–11; 1 Peter 1:6–7*

Keywords: *Companionship; Deliverance; Discipline; Fear; Fear of God; God's Faithfulness; God's Goodness; God's Will; Guidance*

Shrek is a computer-generated, animated film that celebrates the worth of marginalized people in our society. In the film, an ogre named Shrek (voiced by Mike Myers) and a talking donkey (voiced by Eddie Murphy) attempt to rescue a princess (voiced by Cameron Diaz) from a dragon-guarded castle.

On the way to gain freedom for Princess Fiona, Shrek and Donkey come to a rickety wooden bridge that spans a moat of fiery lava. There is no way to reach the castle except to cross the bridge. The fearless ogre doesn't mind the challenge, but Donkey is blind with fear and confesses his fright to his newfound friend.

"You can't tell me you're afraid of heights," Shrek insists, continuing to approach the bridge.

"No," Donkey responds, "I'm just a little uncomfortable about being on a rickety bridge over a boiling lake of lava."

With confidence and compassion, Shrek looks at his little friend and says, "Come on, Donkey. I'm right here beside you for emotional support. We'll just tackle this thing together, one little baby step at a time."

Together they proceed across the bridge with Donkey nervously going first. As they reach the midway point, a rotten plank in the bridge comes loose and falls to the flames below. Donkey loses his concentration and looks down.

"I can't do this!" he insists. "Just let me off right now."

Even though Shrek insists they can do it, the donkey continues to fuss and fume. Shrek, in feigned anger, intentionally swings the suspension bridge back and forth. Outraged by his friend's behavior, Donkey shuffles backwards to escape Shrek's dangerous flailing. Before he knows it, Donkey has walked backwards across the bridge to the castle entrance, and his friend Shrek has safely delivered him to the other side.

Elapsed time: Measured from the beginning of the opening credits, this scene begins at 00:29:37 and lasts approximately one and one-half minutes.

Content: Rated PG for language and scenes of violence

Citation: *Shrek* (DreamWorks, 2001), written by Ted Elliott and Terry Rossio, directed by Andrew Adamson and Vicky Jenson

submitted by Greg Asimakoupoulos, Naperville, Illinois

28. DISCIPLINE

Uncorked

Topic: *When God Takes Things Away*

Texts: *Psalm 39:11; Psalm 119:71; Proverbs 3:11–12;*
Proverbs 11:28; 1 Corinthians 11:29–34;
2 Corinthians 12:7–10; Hebrews 12:5–13;
Revelation 3:19

Keywords: *Ambition; Discipline; Greed; Hardship; Loss;*
Love; Materialism; Selfishness

Uncorked tells the story of an ambitious, self-absorbed man and the futility of seeking wealth. Ross (played by Rufus Sewell) is determined to sell off a priceless family wine collection so that he can buy a local manganese mine and pursue his fortune. His eccentric Uncle Cullen (played by Nigel Hawthorne) is unimpressed by materialism. Taken with the teachings of an early Christian by the name of Simeon, Cullen follows the saint's example by living atop a twenty-cubit-high pillar outside the house and advising his family members to avoid selfish gain.

When Cullen learns of Ross's plans to sell the valuable wine collection, he empties thousands of bottles of wine in the middle of the night. As morning dawns, the housekeeper turns on the kitchen tap and is shocked to find wine flowing out. She lifts the lid of the washing machine and sees clothes submerged in red wine. The emptied contents have infiltrated the estate's water system.

Obviously perplexed, the housekeeper races over a wine-covered walkway to wake Ross up. He bolts to the wine cellar and finds a room littered with uncorked, empty bottles glistening in the sun.

Realizing that his dream has literally gone down the drain, Ross races to the mine and attempts to break in. His uncle meets him. Ross rails against his uncle for destroying the only thing on the estate that had any sellable value—and along with it his dreams.

Ross demands, "What are you doing here? You are trying to destroy my life. Why are you doing this to me?"

Confident that what he did was for his foolish nephew's personal growth, Cullen calmly says, "I'm your uncle, and I love you."

Elapsed time: Beginning with opening credit, scene starts at 00:22:00 and lasts about two and one-half minutes.

Content: Rated PG

Citation: *Uncorked* (Trimark, 2001; previously released as *At Sachem Farm*, 1998), written and directed by John Huddles

submitted by Greg Asimakoupoulos, Naperville, Illinois

29. DREAMS

A Christmas Story

Topic: *Dashed Expectations*

Texts: *Job 6:8; Job 6:20; Job 30:26; Psalm 22:5; Psalm 31:24; Proverbs 13:12; Romans 5:5; Ephesians 3:20*

Keywords: *Ambition; Children; Christmas; Desires; Disappointments; Dreams; Expectations; Frustration; God's Will; Hope; Human Will; Self-Exaltation*

In *A Christmas Story,* young Ralphie (played by Peter Billingsley) wants a Red Ryder BB gun in the worst way. But it seems all adults, including Ralphie's parents, are united in a conspiracy to keep Ralphie from having one. They all cite the same adult rationale: "You'll shoot your eye out!"

On one school day, Ralphie's teacher (played by Tedde Moore) unwittingly provides the perfect opportunity for him to explain the virtues of his Christmas wish. She asks the class to write a theme paper titled "What I Want for Christmas." Ralphie's face practically beams at his good fortune, and he sets out to write the greatest theme paper ever submitted in an elementary school setting.

When he turns his paper in, we hear his thoughts: *I was handing Miss Shields a masterpiece. Maybe Miss Shields in her ecstasy would excuse me from theme writing for the rest of my natural life.* He is convinced he has submitted his magnum opus. Standing at the teacher's desk with a glazed look on his face, he settles into one of his warm, happy fantasies.

Ralphie imagines the teacher reviewing one bad theme paper after another in dramatic disgust, until she finally comes across Ralphie's paper. Skeptical at first, the teacher is soon swept away by Ralphie's submission. *Poetry! Sheer poetry! she exclaims, writing A++++++ across the blackboard as Ralphie is hoisted into the air by his classmates.*

Later, his teacher lays his graded theme paper on his desk. Ralphie is devastated. The grade on his paper is a mediocre C+. And beneath the grade, the teacher had written with red pen, "You'll shoot your eye out."

Elapsed time: Measured from the MGM logo, this scene begins at 00:34:03 and ends at 00:36:33.

Content: Rated PG for profanity

Citation: *A Christmas Story* (MGM, 1983), written by Leigh Brown, Bob Clark, and Jean Shepherd (based on Shepherd's *In God We Trust, All Others Pay Cash*), directed by Bob Clark

submitted by David Slagle, Lawrenceville, Georgia

30. ENEMIES

Ruby Bridges

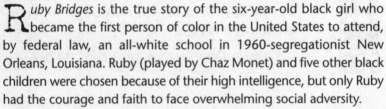

Topic: *Confronting Enemies Courageously*

Texts: *Psalm 16; Luke 23:26–49; Acts 2:22–36; Acts 4:13; Acts 20:22–24; 1 Corinthians 16:13–14*

Keywords: *Abiding in Christ; Adversity; Children; Conflict; Courage; Dependence on God; Enemies; Family; Fathers; Fear; Hatred; Love; Mothers; Persecution; Prayer; Prejudice; Racism; Steadfastness; Strength*

Ruby Bridges is the true story of the six-year-old black girl who became the first person of color in the United States to attend, by federal law, an all-white school in 1960-segregationist New Orleans, Louisiana. Ruby (played by Chaz Monet) and five other black children were chosen because of their high intelligence, but only Ruby had the courage and faith to face overwhelming social adversity.

In one scene, Ruby's father (played by Michael Beach) is concerned about the danger she will face when she walks through the angry crowd of segregationists on her way to enter her school. But her mother (played by Lela Rochon) insists things can only get better if they make them better. "Honey," she tells him, "we can't be afraid."

As Ruby's mother kisses her good-night, she says, "You know Momma's got to go back to work tomorrow. And Daddy's working. So do you think you can be a brave girl and go to school by yourself with the big men?"

Ruby stops smiling and hesitates for a moment, clutching her doll closer. Finally she shrugs a shoulder and agrees, "Okay."

Her mother tries to reassure her, saying, "You know Jesus faced the mob too, baby. Just like you. You know what he did? He prayed for them. Because the Bible says, 'Bless them that persecute you. Bless and curse not.'"

The next day an angry crowd in front of the school waves Confederate flags and hollers, "Go on home!"

Bravely, Ruby steps out of the car with the four federal agents who surround her. One of them reminds her, "Ruby, remember what I told you. Keep looking straight ahead." As they walk through the crowd, one woman spits on the ground; another yells that she is going to hang Ruby.

Ruby's eyes are fixated on a point by the front door as she recalls her parents' words of encouragement: "You are Daddy's brave little girl. Remember, God loves you, Ruby." Suddenly, Ruby is startled as a thrown tomato explodes against a post by the front door. They enter the doors, and dismayed staff members eye her disapprovingly.

Elapsed time: Measured from the beginning of the opening credit, this scene begins at 00:25:00 and ends at 00:28:44.

Content: Not rated

Citation: *Ruby Bridges* (Disney, 1998), written by Toni Ann Johnson, directed by Euzhan Palcy

submitted by Jerry De Luca, Montreal West, Quebec, Canada

31. EVANGELISM

Gettysburg

Topic: *Mission to Set People Free*

Texts: *Luke 4:18; Galatians 5:1; 1 Peter 2:9*

Keywords: *Church; Disciples; Evangelism; Freedom; Purpose; War*

The movie *Gettysburg*, based on *The Killer Angels* by Michael Shaara, brings to life the three bloodiest days of American history. The first scenes take place a couple days before the epic battle at Gettysburg. Colonel Joshua L. Chamberlain (played by Jeff Daniels) of the 20th Maine Regiment learns that his regiment is going to receive 120 Union soldiers who mutinied. Chamberlain is given permission to shoot any of these mutineers who don't cooperate.

Chamberlain tells the men that he's been told about their problem. He admits, "There's nothing I can do today. We're moving out in a few minutes. We'll be moving all day. I've been ordered to take you men with me. I'm told that if you don't come, I can shoot you. Well, you know I won't do that. Maybe somebody else will, but I won't. So, that's that.

"Here's the situation," he continues. "The whole Reb army is up that road a ways, waiting for us. This is no time for an argument. I tell you, we could surely use you fellows. We're now well below half strength. Whether you fight or not, that's up to you. Whether you come along is . . ."

He pauses and then continues, "Well, you're coming. You know who we are. But if you fight alongside of us, there's a few things you must know." Matter-of-factly, he states, "This regiment was formed last summer in Maine. There were a thousand of us then. There are less than three hundred of us now. All of us volunteered to fight for the Union, just as you did. Some came mainly because we were bored at home—thought this looked like it might be fun. Some came because we were ashamed not to. Many of us came because it was the right thing to do. And all of us have seen men die.

"This is a different kind of army. If you look back through history, you'll see men fighting for pay, for women, for some other kind of loot. They fight for land, power, because a king leads them, or just because they like killing. But we are here for something new. This has not happened much in the history of the world. We are an army out to set other men free."

The church is likewise a different kind of army. We are an army out to set other people free.

Elapsed time: Measured from the beginning of the opening credits, this scene begins at 00:25:15 and ends at 00:27:50. On DVD, the scene appears on side 1, chapter 8—"What We're Fighting For."

Content: Rated PG for language and epic battle scenes

Citation: *Gettysburg* (Turner Pictures, 1993), written and directed by Ronald F. Maxwell

submitted by Andrew Miller, Wheaton, Illinois

32. EXAMPLE

Mr. Holland's Opus

Topic: *Reluctant Teacher to Passionate Mentor*

Texts: *Matthew 19:16–22; 1 Corinthians 13:1–3;*
James 1:22; James 2:14–20; 1 John 3:18

Keywords: *Apathy; Christian Life; Church Involvement;*
Discipleship; Example; Ministry; Service; Teachers

Mr. Holland's Opus is a movie about a frustrated young composer in Portland, Oregon, who takes a job as a high school band teacher in the 1960s in order to provide for his family. Diverted from his lifelong goal of achieving critical fame as a classical musician, Glenn Holland (played by Richard Dreyfuss) believes that his school job is only temporary. At first he maintains his determination to write an opus, composing at his piano after the teaching day is over.

He puts in only the minimal number of hours dictated by his teaching contract, and he refuses to attend athletic events or serve as a faculty adviser for student council—anything that would involve him in students' lives. One day between classes, Mrs. Jacobs, the principal (played by Olympia Dukakis), invites Mr. Holland to serve on the textbook committee. He politely but curtly declines, claiming that he's too busy.

Mrs. Jacobs counters, "For a good four or five months now I've been watching you, Mr. Holland. I've never seen a teacher sprint for the parking lot after last period with more speed and enthusiasm than his students. Perhaps you should be our track coach."

"Mrs. Jacobs," Mr. Holland responds defensively, "I get here on time every morning, don't I? I'm doing my job the best I can."

Unwilling to let her rookie teacher off the hook, Mrs. Jacobs continues, "A teacher has two jobs. Fill young minds with knowledge, yes. But more important, give those minds a compass so that knowledge doesn't go to waste. Now, I don't know what you're doing with the knowledge, Mr. Holland. But as a compass, you're stuck."

Eventually, as family demands increase and job pressures multiply, Mr. Holland recognizes that his dream of leaving a lasting musical legacy is merely a dream. But as the years go by, he begins to have a great influence on students. As a music teacher, Mr. Holland uses music to teach his students about life. At the end of the movie, the school board decides to reduce operating costs by cutting music and drama programs. No longer a reluctant band teacher, Mr. Holland passionately defends the role of the arts in public education. Mr. Holland's thirty-five-year career detour changes students' lives.

Elapsed time: Measured from the beginning of the opening credit, this scene begins at 00:21:13 and lasts approximately one minute.

Content: Rated PG for mild profanity

Citation: *Mr. Holland's Opus* (Hollywood Pictures, 1995), written by Patrick Sheane Duncan, directed by Stephen Herek

submitted by Greg Asimakoupoulos, Naperville, Illinois

33. EXPERIENCING GOD

The Preacher's Wife

Topic: *Recognizing God's Help*

Texts: *John 1:1–14; John 9; John 14:6–7; Romans 8:1–4; 1 Timothy 3:16; Hebrews 1:1–2*

Keywords: *Advent; Answers to Prayer; Christmas; Divine Help; Doubt; Experiencing God; Incarnation; Jesus Christ; Prayer; Presence of God*

In the romantic comedy *The Preacher's Wife,* the Reverend Henry Biggs (played by Courtney Vance) doubts his ability to make a difference in a declining community. The Christmas season promises little hope as he fails to keep a community center from closing down, a young church member is jailed after being falsely accused of robbery, and the basement boiler in the church building blows a gasket.

Biggs sits on the edge of his bed in the church parsonage and voices a simple prayer: "Lord, I know you're especially busy this time of year, but I'm just a little tired. If you get a moment, I sure could use some help."

The next day, Biggs carries on with his normal routine. Suddenly an angel (played by Denzel Washington) appears alongside him and announces, "My name's Dudley. I'm here in answer to your request."

Forgetting his earlier prayer, Biggs falters, "My request?"

"For help," Dudley reminds him.

First confused and then amused, Biggs replies, "Is this some kind of joke?"

"Ah, no," responds Dudley. "He doesn't make jokes."

"He?" questions Biggs incredulously.

Dudley looks upward, and Biggs's eyes follow. Dudley explains, "Capital H, capital E. Now I want you to know that the three of us can help you through this little crisis you're having."

Still uncertain of this friendly stranger, Biggs argues, "Look, I don't know who you are . . ."

"Dudley," the angel interrupts.

"Or who put you up to this . . . ," Biggs persists.

Dudley interjects, "He did."

"But I'm afraid you picked the wrong day for me to be a good sport." Biggs then gets in his car and drives away.

People regularly miss God's interventions in life. We don't always recognize God's provision when it comes in a form we don't expect.

Elapsed time: Measured from the beginning of the opening credit, this scene begins at 00:11:49 and runs to 00:13:00.

Content: Rated PG-13 for brief mild profanity

Citation: *The Preacher's Wife* (Touchstone Pictures, 1996), written by Nat Maudlin and Allan Scott (based on a 1947 screenplay by Robert E. Sherwood and Leonardo Bercovici for the film *The Bishop's Wife*), directed by Penny Marshall (based on Robert Nathan's novel *The Bishop's Wife*)

submitted by Clark Cothern, Tecumseh, Michigan

Apollo 13

Topic: *Potential Disaster Becomes NASA's Finest Hour*

Texts: *Psalm 31:24; Psalm 38:15; Psalm 130:7; Jeremiah 17:7; Joel 3:16; Romans 4:18; Galatians 5:5; Hebrews 3:6; Hebrews 11:1*

Keywords: *Adversity; Attitude; Belief; Circumstances and Faith; Confidence; Difficulties; Doubt; Faith; Hope; Optimism; Overcoming; Pessimism; Problems; Trust; Victory*

In April 1970, the Apollo 13 space shuttle was crippled in space, and the astronauts were relying on archaic navigational techniques to get back home. A slight miscalculation could have sent the ship spiraling thousands of miles off course into outer space. Even if the crew could successfully navigate the ship back into earth's orbit, it was feared that the heat shield and the parachutes were not functional. In addition, a tropical storm was brewing in the landing zone. In this scene, a press agent for NASA is asking an official for more information.

As the press agent recounts the multitude of problems to the NASA official, the official, who is clearly stressed, responds, "I know what the problems are, Henry. It will be the worst disaster NASA's ever experienced."

A NASA chief overhears this pessimistic assessment and responds sharply, "With all due respect, I believe this is going to be our finest hour."

A mixture of fear, hope, and pain etches the faces of the NASA team, friends, and family members as they watch for any sign of a successful reentry. Three minutes have passed since the reentry process began. Walter Cronkite's voice informs the viewing audience that no space capsule has taken longer than three minutes to complete reentry. A NASA employee continues to attempt to contact the Odyssey, saying, "Odyssey, this is Houston. Do you read me?" The silence is agonizing. Suddenly the receiver at NASA crackles. A capsule seems to materialize out of thin air on the screen, and the parachutes look like giant flowers that have burst into bloom.

A voice from the Odyssey responds loud and clear, "Hello, Houston. This is Odyssey. It's good to see you again." Friends, family members, and NASA workers erupt in cheers.

Elapsed time: Measured from the Universal logo, this scene begins at 02:03:40 and ends at 02:09:06. Caution: Approximately twenty seconds before this scene begins, one of the astronauts utters a profanity.

Content: Rated PG

Citation: *Apollo 13* (Universal Pictures, 1995), written by William Broyles Jr. and Al Reinert (based on the book *Lost Moon* by Jim Lovell and Jeffrey Kluger), directed by Ron Howard

submitted by David Slagle, Lawrenceville, Georgia

35. FAITH

Contact

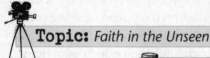

Topic: *Faith in the Unseen*

Texts: *Psalm 19; John 20:24–31; Romans 1:20; Hebrews 11:1–3*

Keywords: *Atheism; Belief; Doubt; Experience; Experiencing God; Faith; Ideologies and Belief Systems; Meaning of Life; Science*

In the 1997 film *Contact*, Dr. Ellie Arroway (played by Jodie Foster) is a radio astronomer trying to fulfill a lifelong quest to discover life on other worlds. The death of her parents, especially her father when she was young, contributed to her rejection of God and her staunch atheism.

Late in the film, radio telescopes pick up a message from space—a plan to build a machine to "transport" one person to make contact with the alien beings. After a long series of events the machine is built, and Ellie is the one chosen to go. She is transported through a wormhole—a tunnel through space and time. She finds herself on a beach, where an alien being appears, having taken the form of her late father so she could feel more comfortable. The alien being tells her that they also are searching for the meaning of life and that, while man is not ready to join the other alien civilizations, this is a first small step.

She is then transported back to the machine and to earth—but in real time, mission control had not observed her to be gone at all. With no proof of her fantastic experience, she must convince the world and an international review panel that she experienced something real. One of the panel members asks her, "Should we take this all on faith?"

"I had an experience I can't prove," she says. "I can't even explain it, but everything that I know as a human being, everything that I am tells me that it was real. I was part of something wonderful, something that changed me forever—a vision of the universe that tells us undeniably how tiny and insignificant and how rare and precious we all are. A vision that tells us we belong to something that is greater than ourselves. That we are not—that none of us are—alone. I wish I could share that. I wish that everyone, if even for one moment, could feel that awe and humility and hope."

Elapsed time: Measured from the Warner Brothers logo, the scene runs from 02:09:00 to 02:18:00.

Content: Rated PG for some mild offensive language and one scene of sensuality. The film, based on the novel by the late scientist and atheist Carl Sagan, gives equal treatment to the need for faith and the search for truth by both science and religion.

Citation: *Contact* (Warner Brothers, 1997), written by James V. Hart and Michael Goldenberg (based on the novel by Carl Sagan), directed by Robert Zemeckis

submitted by Jerry De Luca, Montreal West, Quebec, Canada

36. FAITH

The Empire Strikes Back

Topic: *Impossibility Thinking*

Texts: *Deuteronomy 18:10–14; Zechariah 10:2; Matthew 24:5; Acts 2:1–21; 1 Timothy 4:1*

Keywords: *Belief; Faith; False Doctrine; False Gods; False Religions; False Teaching; Miracles; New Age; Occult; Religion; Self-Reliance; Supernatural Experiences*

In George Lucas's *The Empire Strikes Back,* which has a pervasive New Age worldview but illustrates some biblical principles, nine-hundred-year-old Master Jedi-Knight Yoda (voiced by Frank Oz) counsels Jedi-hopeful Luke Skywalker (played by Mark Hamill) on how to use the Force so he can be victorious in the ongoing battles against the evil Darth Vader and the imperialistic Empire. While teaching Luke to use the Force on the isolated planet Dagobah, Yoda challenges him to balance himself upside down on one hand with Yoda perched on one of Luke's feet. Simultaneously, Luke must mentally raise a basketball-sized rock in the air.

Yoda tells him, "Use the Force. . . . Now—the stone. Feel it."

Suddenly, Luke is distracted by the sound of his starship, almost half sunk, now sinking to the muddy lake's bottom. He falls forward, and Yoda tumbles down. Seeing only the tip of his ship's wing sticking out from the swamp, Luke despairs. "We'll never get it out now!"

Yoda sighs and answers, "So certain are you? Always with you it cannot be done. Hear you nothing that I say?"

"Master, moving stones around is one thing. This is totally different."

Yoda insists, "No! No different! Only different in your mind. You must unlearn what you have learned."

Luke nods, "All right, I'll give it a try."

Yoda, somewhat exasperated, says "No! Try not. Do. Or do not. There is no try."

Luke tries to mentally raise the ship out of the water using the Force but fails miserably. Exhausted by the effort, he sits down beside Yoda and tells him, "I can't. It's too big."

Yoda answers, "Size matters not. Look at me. Judge me by my size, do you?" Yoda tells Luke that his ally is the Force, and it is a powerful ally: "Life creates it, makes it grow. Its energy surrounds us and binds us. . . . You must feel the Force around you. Here, between you . . . me . . . the tree . . . the rock . . . everywhere! Yes, even between this land and that ship!"

Luke, totally dejected, tells him, "You want the impossible."

Yoda concentrates and mentally raises the ship out of the water and onto the shore. Luke walks around the ship in amazement and tells Yoda, "I don't—I don't believe it!"

Yoda responds, "That is why you fail."

Elapsed time: Measured from the beginning of the opening credit, this scene begins at 01:07:35 and ends at 01:12:50.

Content: Rated PG for violence

Citation: *The Empire Strikes Back* (20th Century Fox, 1980), written by Leigh Brackett and Lawrence Kasdan (based on a story by George Lucas), directed by Irvin Kershner

submitted by Jerry De Luca, Montreal West, Quebec, Canada

37. FAITH

Indiana Jones and the Last Crusade

Topic: *Taking a Step of Faith*

Texts: *Psalm 32:10; Psalm 33:18–19; Psalm 84; Proverbs 3:5; Jeremiah 17:7; Jeremiah 39:18; Matthew 21:21–22; Mark 9:23; Mark 11:23–24; Luke 7:50; Romans 4; 2 Corinthians 5:7; Hebrews 11; 1 Peter 1:8*

Keywords: *Belief; Difficulties; Faith; Risk; Seen and Unseen; Trust; Trustworthiness of God; Uncertainties; Visible and Invisible*

Indiana Jones (played by Harrison Ford) is a daring archaeologist who travels the world in search of great treasures. In *Indiana Jones and the Last Crusade,* Indiana sets out with his father (played by Sean Connery) to find the Holy Grail.

As they are closing in on the Grail, Indiana's father is mortally wounded in a gunfight. The search for the Grail takes on new intensity for Indiana, because it reportedly can bring healing to those who drink from it.

With his father groaning in the background, Indiana follows an ancient book that gives clues to guide him through a maze of obstacles to the place where the Grail is hidden. He comes to the brink of a chasm deeper than the eye can see. He sees a path continuing on the other side of the chasm, but there is no bridge to get across.

Indiana's face falls as he is faced with the impossible. Exasperated, he looks in vain for another way to cross. All he sees is the sheer cliff edge and the vast gulf beneath him. Then, as he studies his guide-book, his face relaxes in realization, and he says, "It's a leap of faith."

With his father whispering, "You must believe, boy, you must believe," Indiana sets his eyes, gathers his courage, and slowly raises one foot into the empty air in front of him.

"Thud!" He lands on solid ground, and the camera pans sideways to show Indiana standing on a narrow rock bridge, deceptively carved to match the exact outline of the ravine beneath it.

Overcome with relief, he quickly crosses the chasm and goes on to discover the Grail on the other side.

Elapsed time: Measured from the beginning of the opening credit, this scene begins at 01:46:50 and ends at 01:48:45.

Content: Rated PG-13 for violence

Citation: *Indiana Jones and the Last Crusade* (Lucasfilm/Paramount, 1989), written by Jeffrey Boam (based on a story by George Lucas and Menno Meyjes), directed by Steven Spielberg

submitted by Bill White, Paramount, California

38. FAITHFULNESS

Mr. Holland's Opus

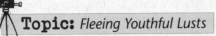

Topic: *Fleeing Youthful Lusts*

Texts: *Exodus 20:14; Deuteronomy 5:18; Proverbs 5; Proverbs 6:23–25; Matthew 4:1–11; 2 Timothy 2:22; James 4:7*

Keywords: *Adultery; Choices; Faithfulness; Marriage; Men; Purity; Self-Denial; Sin; Temptation*

Mr. Holland's Opus is a movie about a frustrated young composer in Portland, Oregon, who takes a job as a high school band teacher in the 1960s in order to provide for his family. Diverted from his lifelong goal of achieving critical fame as a classical musician, Glenn Holland (played by Richard Dreyfuss) believes that his school job is only temporary. At first he maintains his determination to write an opus, composing at his piano after putting in a full day teaching. But as family demands increase and job pressures multiply, Mr. Holland recognizes that his dream of leaving a lasting musical legacy is merely a dream.

Throughout the movie, Mr. Holland's relationship with his wife (played by Glenne Headley) is in throes, due in part to the challenges of raising a deaf son. While directing the school musical, the middle-aged teacher is intrigued by the musical skill and physical beauty of a senior named Rowena (played by Jean Louisa Kelly). As Mr. Holland affirms her abilities, Rowena becomes attracted to him. She tells her teacher that she has decided to move to New York City in pursuit of her own dreams, but she wants him to go with her. Rowena tempts him with the chance to escape the constraints of his current life and finally be able to write music. After the final performance of the musical, Mr. Holland meets her at the local drugstore, where the bus picks up passengers. Her eyes light up as she sees him approach, but then she notices that he has no luggage.

"You pack light," she jests.

Mr. Holland doesn't acknowledge her attempt at humor but hands her a slip of paper with the name of a couple he knows in New York where she can stay.

"This isn't the way I imagined it," Rowena reluctantly admits.

"But it's the best way," Mr. Holland says, finding the inner strength to resist temptation.

That evening, Mr. Holland walks into his bedroom where his wife appears to be sleeping. He looks tenderly at her and says, "I love you." His wife looks up at him and responds, "I know." Aware of the victory he has won by honoring his wedding vows, he takes his wife in his arms and holds her.

Elapsed time: Measured from the beginning of the opening credit, this scene begins at 01:40:36 and lasts approximately four and one-half minutes.

Content: Rated PG for mild profanity

Citation: *Mr. Holland's Opus* (Hollywood Pictures, 1995), written by Patrick Sheane Duncan, directed by Stephen Herek

submitted by Greg Asimakoupoulos, Naperville, Illinois

39. FATHERHOOD

The Parent Trap

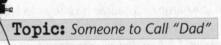

Topic: *Someone to Call "Dad"*

Texts: *Psalm 2:7; Psalm 68:5; Isaiah 64:8; Matthew 6:8–9; John 20:17; Romans 8:14–16; Galatians 3:26–29; Galatians 4:6–7; Hebrews 12:9; 1 John 3:1*

Keywords: *Divorce; Family; Fatherhood; Fatherhood of God; Parenting*

In the 1998 Disney movie *The Parent Trap,* identical twins who were separated at birth by their parents' divorce accidentally meet eleven years later at summer camp. Together the twins plan to switch identities so each can meet the respective parent she's never known and try to bring their parents together again.

As Annie (played by Lindsay Lohan), who is pretending to be Hallie, disembarks from her plane, her father (played by Dennis Quaid) is waiting for her. Annie is tentative but exuberant as she sees him and says, "Oh, gosh, it's him."

"Get into these arms, you little punk!" her dad says.

She runs to embrace him with a big smile, saying, "Dad! Finally!" The father tells her he missed her and a lot had been happening. Annie responds, "A lot's been happening to me too, Dad. I mean, I feel I'm practically a new woman!"

As they're walking to the car, the father notices that she can't stop looking at him and asks, "What? Did I cut myself shaving?"

Annie answers, "No. It's just seeing you for the first time. I mean, you know, in so long."

As they drive toward his home, Annie talks about the camp, ending almost all her sentences with the word *Dad.* He asks her, "Why do you keep saying *Dad* at the end of every sentence?"

Annie answers, "I'm sorry, I didn't realize I was doing it, Dad. Sorry, Dad." They both laugh. "Do you want to know why I keep saying *Dad?* The truth?"

The father says, "Because you missed your old man so much, right?"

"Exactly. It's because in my whole life—I mean, you know, for the past eight weeks—I was never able to say the word *Dad.* Never. Not once. And if you ask me, a dad is an irreplaceable person in a girl's life. Think about it. There's a whole day devoted to celebrating fathers. Just imagine someone's life without a father. Never buying a Father's Day card. Never sitting on their father's lap. Or being able to say 'Hi, Dad,' or, 'What's up, Dad?' or, 'Catch you later, Dad.' I mean, a baby's first words are always *Da-da,* aren't they?"

The father asks, "Let me see if I get this. You missed being able to call me *Dad?*"

Annie answers, "Yeah, I really have, Dad."

Elapsed time: This scene begins at 00:44:50 and ends at 00:48:18. Warning: Almost immediately following the scene, Annie exclaims, "O my God!" as they drive up to her father's spacious ranch.

Content: Rated PG

Citation: *The Parent Trap* (Walt Disney Pictures, 1998; remake of a 1961 film), written by Nancy Meyers and Charles Shyer from the original 1961 screenplay by David Swift (based on Erich Kastner's book *Das Doppelte Lottchen*), directed by Nancy Meyers

submitted by Jerry De Luca, Montreal West, Quebec, Canada

40. FATHERHOOD OF GOD

Field of Dreams

Topic: *Reconciling with the Father*

Texts: *Exodus 20:12; Luke 15:11–24; Romans 5:9–11; 2 Corinthians 5:18–21; Ephesians 2:14–18; Colossians 1:19–22*

Keywords: *Fatherhood of God; Fathers; Grief; Heaven; Reconciliation; Regret; Relationships; Separation*

Field of Dreams is a fantasy-drama about baseball, the pursuit of a dream, and reconciliation between a father and son. Though the film borders on the thoroughly unbelievable (with a "voice" talking from a cornfield, old baseball players walking in and out of a center-field "heaven," and time travel back to a town in 1972), it somehow gets us to suspend our disbelief because of its thematic realism.

Ray Kinsella (played by Kevin Costner) is on the way to reconciling with his long-dead father—though he doesn't know it yet. About halfway through the movie he's driving his rustic, red, Volkswagen van down back roads in the heart of the Midwest, the gently sloping hills and cornfields passing by. Sitting next to Ray is his newfound friend Terrence (played by James Earl Jones). The two men have just picked up an adolescent hitchhiker who tells them, "I'm a baseball player." It sparks a conversation about Ray and his father—and the role that baseball once played in their relationship.

"What happened to your father?" Terrence asks.

"He never made it as a ballplayer," says Ray, "so he tried to get his son to make it for him. By the time I was ten, playing baseball got to be like eating vegetables or taking out the garbage. So when I was fourteen, I started to refuse. Can you believe that? An American boy refusing to play catch with his father?"

Ray goes on to talk about the pain of the ever-widening rift that grew between them until one day it resulted in a complete and permanent separation. "When I was seventeen, I packed my things, said something awful, and left. After a while, I wanted to come home, but I didn't know how. . . . Made it back for the funeral, though."

Sadness and regret pervade the atmosphere as the van continues down the road.

But in the extended closing scene of the movie, Ray Kinsella is miraculously allowed to meet his dead father, John Kinsella. They meet on a baseball field that Ray has constructed in a cornfield on his Iowa farm. Ray stands along the sidelines with his wife, Annie. They turn their gaze to home plate. There, standing with his back to them and pulling off his old-fashioned catcher's equipment, is a young man dressed in a loosely fitting uniform he once wore as a minor leaguer.

Suddenly it dawns on Ray that he is witnessing a miracle of monumental proportions. He soon shakes hands with John Kinsella, his own father, returned from "baseball heaven." They talk for a while, and then the father begins to walk away. Ray calls out: "Hey, Dad, want to play catch?"

"I'd like that," says the father.

They walk onto the field together—Ray standing by home plate, his father out on the pitcher's mound—and they begin tossing the ball back and forth. There is a gleam in their eyes; no words need be spoken.

Elapsed time: Measured from the initial flashing of the studio symbol, the car scene begins at 01:11:15 and ends at 01:13:40, and the reconciliation scene begins at 01:34:00 and ends as the closing credits begin to roll.

Content: Rated PG—an excellent family-oriented film that conveys the value of family life, doing what's right, and reconciling differences in family relationships. However, there is a reference in the opening scene to marijuana usage, as well as a few occasions of mildly offensive language.

Citation: *Field of Dreams* (Universal Pictures, 1989), written and directed by Phil Alden Robinson (based on the novel *Shoeless Joe* by W. P. Kinsella)

submitted by Gary Wilde, Oviedo, Florida

41. FEER

First Knight

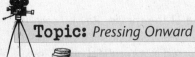

Topic: *Pressing Onward*

Texts: *Matthew 14:25–32; Philippians 3:12–14; Hebrews 10:36*

Keywords: *Boldness; Challenges; Courage; Difficulties; Faith; Fear; Overcoming*

Based on Arthurian legend, *First Knight* chronicles the rise of Lancelot (played by Richard Gere) to the round table of King Arthur (played by Sean Connery) and their fight against the renegade knight Malagant.

During Arthur and Guinevere's wedding celebration, guests participate in the challenge of the Gauntlet. The Gauntlet is an elevated obstacle course comprised of a hundred moving parts, including whirling balls and swinging blades. No one has ever successfully navigated the Gauntlet before, but the young men line up for the chance to run the course. The prize for making it through is a place of honor at Arthur's table and a kiss from the queen. The young men suit up in huge padded outfits to protect themselves and then hurtle through the course.

The first three men attempt the Gauntlet—and all fail. One by one, they misjudge the course and are swept aside. When the queen promises a kiss to whomever makes it through the Gauntlet, Lancelot begins climbing the platform without a single pad. With cries of "You're mad! You'll kill yourself!" from the crowd, Lancelot continues.

His first obstacle is a set of huge swirling balls, which he dodges with graceful timing, correctly judging each threat and carefully moving ahead. Next, he leaps up to grab one of the spinning wheels from which the balls were suspended. He rides the wheel around to the other side, creatively circumventing another set of obstacles. He then faces his biggest threat—dozens of blades slicing through his path. He inches past blade after blade, and at a crucial point he pauses long for just the right opening. Finally, he plunges forward headfirst and dashes to safety. The king and crowd wildly applaud him.

Later, Lancelot tells the king how he successfully navigated the Gauntlet: "It's not hard to know where the danger is if you watch it coming. Perhaps fear made them [the others who failed] go back when they should have gone forward."

Elapsed time: Measured from the beginning of the opening scene, the scene of the men failing begins at 00:36:45 and lasts approximately one and one-half minutes. The scene of Lancelot entering the Gauntlet begins at 00:38:15 and lasts approximately two minutes.

Content: Rated PG-13 for violent medieval battles

Citation: *First Knight* (Columbia, 1995), written by William Nicholson (based on a story by Lorne Cameron, David Hoselton, and William Nicholson), directed by Jerry Zucker

submitted by Bill White, Paramount, California

42. FORGIVENESS

The Mission

Topic: *Power of Grace*

Texts: *John 3:16; Romans 3:21–26; Romans 5:6–8; Ephesians 1:7; Colossians 1:21–22*

Keywords: *Despair; Forgiveness; Grace; Guilt; Hope; Mercy; Redemption; Regret*

The Mission tells the story of a Jesuit priest named Gabriel and a mercenary named Mendoza. In about 1750, Gabriel is commissioned to build a mission in South America for the Guarani Indians.

On the way, Gabriel (played by Jeremy Irons) meets with Mendoza (played by Robert De Niro), who has been a slave trader. He has made slaves of some of the Guarani people. Mendoza also killed his brother in a jealous rage over a woman, and he is now inconsolable, trapped in a prison of guilt and regret. Gabriel attempts to persuade the guilt-stricken man to accompany him to the Guarani village where he has committed so many of his sins.

Speaking words of hope, Gabriel says, "There is life."

The slave trader counters, "There is no life!"

Gabriel says, "There is a way out, Mendoza."

"For me there is no redemption," Mendoza says.

Gabriel says, "God gave us the burden of freedom. You chose your crime; do you have the courage to choose your penance? Do you dare do that?"

"There is no penance hard enough for me."

"But do you dare try it?"

"Do I dare? Do you dare to see it fail?"

As they begin the arduous journey, the priest straps a huge sack of armor on Mendoza's back. To reach the village the men must travel over cliffs and waterfalls. What would be perilous for the most experienced hiker is virtually impossible for someone with a hundred-pound sack of armor strapped to his back.

When they finally reach their destination, the Guarani people are excited to see Gabriel. But as they recognize Mendoza, it becomes a moment of truth. One of the men unsheathes a knife and holds it to Mendoza's neck. Mendoza remains calm, prepared to receive the punishment he deserves for his sins.

In an unexpected portrait of grace, the Guarani removes his knife from Mendoza's throat and cuts free the pack of armor. All watch as it falls from the slave trader's back and clatters down the mountainside into a ravine below. Mendoza, shocked and confused, begins to sob uncontrollably and clings to the Indian man's feet in contrition.

Elapsed time: Measured from the beginning of the opening credit, this scene begins at 00:36:29 and lasts about six minutes.

Content: Rated PG

Citation: *The Mission* (Warner Brothers and Enigma, 1986), written by Robert Bolt, directed by Roland Joffé

submitted by Greg Asimakoupoulos, Naperville, Illinois, and Doug Scott, Elgin, Illinois

43. FRIENDSHIP

It's a Wonderful Life

Topic: *Supportive Fellowship*

Texts: *Psalm 112:5; Proverbs 11:24; Proverbs 22:9; Matthew 10:8; Matthew 19:21; Mark 10:21; Luke 3:11; Luke 6:38; Acts 2:42–47; Acts 4:32; Acts 20:35; Romans 12:13*

Keywords: *Caring; Church; Community; Compassion; Devotion; Family; Fellowship; Friendship; Generosity; Giving; Human Help; Love; Loyalty; Money; Self-Sacrifice*

The movie *It's a Wonderful Life* celebrates one man's extraordinary generosity. George Bailey (played by James Stewart), the proprietor of a building and loan institution, demonstrates compassion, hope, and trust in others—even when adversity strikes.

The trouble began when George's absentminded uncle misplaced $8,000. George realized he could go to jail for his uncle's mistake, and he wished he'd never been born. But then Clarence Oddbody, an angel (played by Henry Travers), was dispatched from heaven to show George what the world would have been like had he never been born. George discovered that, in spite of his financial woes, he was a wealthy man because of the investments he had made all his life in other people.

George then returned to the real world, grateful to be alive. Even though the law wanted him for the missing $8,000, George was thrilled to know that he served a purpose in life. As he entered the front door of his home, he saw the bank examiner and the sheriff awaiting him. Eyeing his children, George ran to hug and kiss them.

Mary, his wife, entered through the door, and he greeted her with a loving embrace. "You have no idea what happened to me," he said.

Mary responded, "You have no idea what happened while you were gone."

Hearing the commotion of an approaching crowd, she motioned for him to stand in front of the decorated Christmas tree in the living room. Uncle Billy was first to enter the house, carrying a wicker basket filled with cash. He dumped it all out on a table in front of George and explained, "Mary told some people you were in trouble, and they scattered all over town collecting money. They didn't ask any questions. They just wanted to help."

People then filled the living room and piled money on the table. Mr. Martini, the owner of the local nightclub, brought in money from the jukebox. Mr. Gower, the druggist George worked for as a boy, brought in all his accounts receivable funds. Millionaire Sam Wainwright, a lifelong friend, sent a telegram promising cash to cover the missing money. George's war-hero brother entered and proposed a toast: "To my brother, the richest man in town."

George eyed a copy of a book on top of the pile of money. He opened it up and discovered that it was a gift from Clarence, the angel. The inscription read as follows: "No man is a failure who has friends."

Elapsed time: Measured from the beginning of the opening credit, this scene begins at 02:02:58 and lasts approximately six and one-half minutes.

Content: Rated G

Citation: *It's a Wonderful Life* (Liberty Films/RKO Radio Pictures, 1946), written by Frances Goodrich, Albert Hackett, Jo Swerling, and Frank Capra (based on "The Greatest Gift," a short story written by Philip Van Doren Stern), directed by Frank Capra

submitted by Greg Asimakoupoulos, Naperville, Illinois

44. GENEROSITY

It's a Wonderful Life

Topic: *Generosity in Action*

Texts: *Psalm 112:5; Proverbs 11:24; Matthew 10:8; Matthew 19:21; Mark 10:21; Luke 3:11; Luke 6:38; Acts 20:35; Romans 12:13; Ephesians 4:28; 1 Timothy 6:18; 1 John 3:17*

Keywords: *Caring; Community; Compassion; Consideration; Generosity; Giving; Human Help; Love; Money; Need; Self-Sacrifice; Unselfishness*

The classic film *It's a Wonderful Life* celebrates the significance of one man's contribution to his community. George Bailey (played by James Stewart) consistently demonstrates self-denial and generosity. A proprietor of a loan institution, George helps families through tough Depression-era times.

Bailey's Building and Loan is put in jeopardy by George's uncle, who misplaces $8,000, and George realizes he could go to jail. He wishes he'd never been born. But Clarence Oddbody, an angel dispatched from heaven, shows George what the world would have been like had he never been born.

Early in the movie, George marries his sweetheart, Mary (played by Donna Reed), on Black Tuesday in October 1929. The stock market has just collapsed. En route to the train station, the cab driver calls attention to a crowd clamoring for their money at the Bedford Falls Bank. Fearing a similar scene at the family business, George asks to stop by the Bailey Building and Loan.

George jumps out of the cab and finds a crowd of people waiting at a locked door. The stock market collapse has motivated his clients to try to withdraw their money. Though perplexed about what to do, George opens the door and lets in his friends, who demand their money at once. George attempts to calm the crowd, all the while knowing that he doesn't have sufficient cash on hand to honor everyone's request.

George tries to calm the crowd, saying, "We can get through this thing all right. We've got to stick together, though. We've got to have faith in each other."

An elderly woman responds, "But my husband hasn't worked in over a year. I need money."

Just in time, George's new bride has an idea. Retrieving the honeymoon nest egg from her purse, she holds up the money and asks, "How much do you need?"

Immediately, George announces, "I've got $2,000. This should tide us over."

One man insists on withdrawing all $200 from his account. George pleads with him not to be greedy, so that the money can go further. Several others ask for more modest amounts. As the time approaches 6:00 P.M., George and Uncle Billy count down the waning moments that will close out the business day: "5—4—3—2—1 . . . Bingo!"

Uncle Billy beams, "We're going to make it, George. They'll never close us up today."

A grateful George responds, "We made it! We're still in business." Holding up two solitary dollar bills, he adds, "And with two bucks to spare."

Elapsed time: Measured from the beginning of the opening credit, this scene begins at 00:54:29 and lasts approximately four minutes.

Content: Rated G

Citation: *It's a Wonderful Life* (Liberty Films/RKO Radio Pictures, 1946), written by Frances Goodrich, Albert Hackett, Jo Swerling, and Frank Capra (based on "The Greatest Gift," a short story written by Philip Van Doren Stern), directed by Frank Capra

submitted by Greg Asimakoupoulos, Naperville, Illinois

45. GOSPEL

Amistad

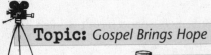

Topic: *Gospel Brings Hope*

Texts: *Psalm 43; Romans 8:17–18; Galatians 3:28–29; Hebrews 11:1*

Keywords: *Afterlife; Attitudes and Emotions; Bible; Cross; Despair; Gospel; Heaven; Hope; Jesus Christ; Resurrection; Suffering*

The movie *Amistad* is about a slave ship filled with abducted African men, women, and children. In the face of starvation, beatings, rape, and murder, the Africans plan a coup en route from Africa to Cuba. On a stormy night, their leader, Cinque (played by Djimon Hounsou), unshackles his comrades. They seize the ship and order the planter to sail them back to Africa.

Instead of navigating them to Africa, however, the planter lands them at an eastern American seaport, where the Africans are imprisoned.

On the eve of the judge's verdict, the Africans are scattered about their prison cell, lost in despondency. But one sits contentedly in a corner reading a Bible given by a missionary.

Cinque, the fearless leader, glumly looks over at a fellow captive, Yamba (played by Raazaq Adoti), and says, "You don't have to pretend to be interested in that. Nobody's watching but me."

But Yamba is authentically engrossed in the book. Momentarily, he glances up from it and says, "I'm not pretending. I'm beginning to understand it." Though the Bible is written in English, a language Yamba does not understand, its vivid illustrations speak to him.

Intrigued, Cinque scoots over to read the narrative depicted by the black-and-white sketches. Wanting to share what he has learned, Yamba begins to tell the story in their native tongue. "Their people have suffered more than ours." Referring to a picture of Jews being attacked by lions, he continues, "Their lives were full of suffering."

Yamba flips the page and eagerly points to a picture of the infant Jesus, crowned with a halo of light, "Then he was born and everything changed."

Cinque asks, "Who is he?"

Yamba doesn't know who the child is, but he knows that he must be special. Referring to a picture of Jesus haloed by the sun, riding on a donkey, and being praised by onlookers, Yamba tells Cinque, "Everywhere he goes, he is followed by the sun."

Yamba skips to other pictures of Jesus to prove his point. The celestial light engulfs him as he heals people with his hands, as he protects an outcast woman, as he embraces a mob of children.

But this is not the end of the story. Yamba explains, "Something happened. He was captured, accused of some crime."

Cinque shakes his head back and forth and insists, "He must have done something."

Yamba says, "Why? What did *we* do?" Still gazing at the picture, Yamba asks, "Do you want to see how they killed him?"

Sensing Yamba's emotional breakdown, Cinque reminds him, "This is just a story, Yamba."

Yamba shakes his head in protest. This man's death was real. With renewed enthusiasm he turns the page and joyfully explains to Cinque, "But look. That's not the end of it. His people took his body down from . . ." Yamba pauses and draws a cross in the air.

Yamba says, "They took him into a cave. They wrapped him in cloth, like we do. They thought he was dead, but he appeared before his people again—and he spoke to them." Peace settles over Yamba. Looking at Cinque he says, "Then, finally, he rose into the sky."

Gazing intently at Cinque, Yamba insists, "This is where the soul goes when you die here. This is where we're going when they kill us." Stroking a picture that depicts heaven, Yamba concludes, "It doesn't look so bad."

Elapsed time: Measured from when the DreamWorks logo appears, the scene begins at 01:35:30 and lasts four minutes.

Content: Rated R for some violence and for showing the Africans nude as they are transported

Citation: *Amistad* (DreamWorks, 1997), written by David Franzoni, directed by Steven Spielberg

submitted by Melissa Parks, Des Plaines, Illinois

46. GRACE

Pay It Forward

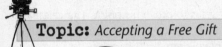

Topic: *Accepting a Free Gift*

Texts: *Matthew 10:8; John 3:16; Romans 3:22–24; Romans 5:8; Ephesians 2:8–10*

Keywords: *Accepting Christ; Christ's Love; Gift of Salvation; God's Goodness; Grace; Righteousness by Faith; Salvation by Grace; Suspicion; Unbelief; Works*

In *Pay It Forward*, reporter Chris Chandler (played by Jay Mohr) arrives in a residential neighborhood that is the scene of an ongoing hostage situation. As he begins to question the police, the hostage-taker crashes through the garage door of the home in a large SUV and rams into Chandler's vintage Mustang, which is parked on the street. The police take off in hot pursuit, leaving Chandler alone to bemoan his mangled car.

As he laments, a well-groomed lawyer appears beside him. The lawyer asks if Chandler would like his brand-new Jaguar. Chandler thanks the lawyer for the opportunity to borrow his car.

"No, it's yours," the lawyer says. He tells Chandler he's had a run of luck lately, and he doesn't need it; Chandler can have it.

Chandler can't believe it. Even as the lawyer walks away in the rain, Chandler shouts after him, calling him a freak for giving him the car. He protests that he doesn't really need a car, and he even suspects that the Jaguar is rigged with explosives.

But it isn't. It is a perfectly beautiful new car—and it is a gift.

Elapsed time: This scene begins one minute into the movie and lasts approximately two minutes.

Content: Rated PG-13 for vulgarity and profanity

Citation: *Pay It Forward* (Warner Brothers, 2000), written by Leslie Dixon (based on the novel *Pay It Forward* by Catherine Ryan Hyde), directed by Mimi Leder

submitted by Carey Nieuwhof, Ontario, Canada

47. HARDSHIP

O Brother, Where Art Thou?

Topic: *Foxhole Faith*

Texts: *Psalm 78:18–22; Psalm 107; Matthew 7:7–8*

Keywords: *Doubt; Experiencing God; Faith; Forsaking God; Hardship; Miracles; Prayer; Science; Seeking God; Signs and Wonders; Skepticism; Unbelief*

O*Brother, Where Art Thou?* is a comedy based on Homer's *The Odyssey*, set in Depression-era America. The story revolves around three men, all imprisoned for crimes that range from petty larceny to grand theft, who escape from a chain gang. Ulysses (played by George Clooney), the leader of the escaped convicts, encourages the escape by telling his companions about a buried treasure. Ulysses explains that before he was arrested for bank robbery, he buried the stolen loot in his hometown. Promising an equal split, Ulysses convinces the two men to whom he is chained to make a run for it.

While on the run, the three men meet a grizzled old man operating a manually powered cart on the railroad tracks. The man speaks in strange riddles. Unsolicited, the old man begins to prophesy. He says, "You will find a fortune, though it will not be the fortune you seek." Among many other cryptic things, he says, "You will see a cow on a roof."

Ulysses, an incurable skeptic of anything that smacks of the supernatural, scoffs at the prophecy. Admittedly, the prophecy does seem a little silly—until the end of the movie when Ulysses and his two friends do not get the treasure they set out to recover. Instead, the governor of the state grants them a pardon—a fortune they weren't seeking.

Unfortunately, a posse—not having heard the news of the pardon—apprehends them. About to be hanged, Ulysses, Delmer, and Pete stand trembling in a lonely wooded area, far away from anyone who can help them. They look hopelessly up at the three ropes that hang from an old tree branch. Ulysses, to this point an agnostic, drops to his knees and begins to pray for miraculous intervention: "Lord, please look down and recognize this poor sinner. Please, Lord, I just want to see my daughters again.... I know I've been guilty of pride and short dealing. I know I've turned my back on you.... Help us, Lord."

As Ulysses ends his prayer, a small stream of water appears out of nowhere. The others notice the water also and stare at it with a look of confusion. Suddenly, a mighty rush of water sweeps away everyone and everything in its path. After a few moments, Ulysses, Delmer, and Pete bob to the surface, gasping for air. Delmer proclaims, "It's a miracle! We prayed to God, and he pitied us!"

Ulysses, who moments earlier was crying out to God for just such a miracle, chastises his "hayseed" cohorts for attributing their salvation to the miraculous. He says, "Don't be ignorant. There's a perfectly scientific explanation for what just happened." When Pete reminds him of his prayer, Ulysses responds, "Well, any human being will cast about in times of stress." He then turns to see a cow seeking refuge from the flood on the roof of a house.

God, a sought-after friend in times of calamity, is often abandoned in times of peace.

Elapsed time: Measured from the beginning of the opening credit, this scene begins at 01:36:00 and goes to 01:40:08.

Content: Rated PG-13 for profanity and vulgarity

Citation: *O Brother, Where Art Thou?* (Touchstone, 2000), written by Joel and Ethan Coen (roughly based on Homer's *The Odyssey*), directed by Joel Coen

submitted by David Slagle, Lawrenceville, Georgia

48. HEAVEN

Annie

Topic: Warbucks's Mansion Like Heaven to Annie

Texts: Isaiah 61:3; Matthew 5:12; Luke 6:38; Luke 23:43; John 14:3; Ephesians 3:20; Jude 24; Revelation 7:17; Revelation 21:4; Revelation 22:12

Keywords: Eternal Life; Eternal Perspective; Gift of Salvation; Grace; Heaven; Paradise; Rest

Annie tells the adventures of an orphan girl at the Hudson Street Home for Girls in New York City during the Great Depression. Miss Hannigan (played by Carol Burnett), the alcoholic proprietor, makes life miserable for the girls under her charge. She forces them in the middle of the night to scrub floors, sew piecework strips of fabric, peel potatoes, and wash the mildew-soiled walls. "These floors better shine like the top of the Chrysler Building before breakfast, or your rear ends will!" Miss Hannigan roars.

The children dream of being adopted to escape the dismal environment of the orphanage.

Annie (played by Aileen Quinn) gets her escape when billionaire philanthropist Oliver Warbucks (played by Albert Finney) decides to borrow her for a week to improve his public image. His secretary, Grace Farrell (played by Ann Reinking), retrieves Annie from the orphanage and escorts her to his mansion, where the little girl is agog with fascination. She walks through the massive entryway and is amazed at the beauty. There are immense floral displays, massive balconies, spiral staircases, and a full-length, stained-glass window on the ceiling. She feels like she has died and gone to heaven.

Grace asks, "Well, Annie, what would you like to do first?"

Accustomed to housework at the orphanage, Annie looks around with her hand on her chin and responds, "Well, I could do the windows first, then the floors. That way if I drip . . ."

Grace interrupts her and says with a smile, "Annie, you don't understand. You won't have to do any cleaning while you're with us. You're our guest."

A big smile crosses Annie's face. One after another of the maids and butlers curtsy in her presence. One will pick out her clothes. Another will draw her bath. Yet another will turn down her bed. It is a dream come true. This is a life far beyond anything the little girl has ever imagined. As the maids and butlers dance around the room and prepare the banquet table for an enormous feast, all Annie can say is, "I think I'm going to like it here!"

Elapsed time: Measured from the beginning of the opening credit, this scene begins at 00:30:00 and lasts approximately four minutes.

Content: Rated G

Citation: *Annie* (Columbia Pictures, 1982; film version of the original stage musical *Annie*), written by Harold Gray (comic strip "Little Orphan Annie"), Thomas Meehan (stage version), and Carol Sobieski (film version), directed by John Huston

submitted by Greg Asimakoupoulos, Naperville, Illinois

49. HELP FROM GOD

The Legend of Bagger Vance

Topic: *Finding Your Purpose*

Texts: *Deuteronomy 30:19; Joshua 24:15; Jeremiah 29:11; Galatians 5:1; Ephesians 2:10; Philippians 1:6; Philippians 2:12–13; Philippians 3:7–14; 1 Peter 2:9*

Keywords: *Choices; Decisions; Destiny; Help from God; Past; Predestination; Purpose; Repentance; Strength*

The Legend of Bagger Vance is a movie about a mythical golf match set in the 1930s in Savannah, Georgia, involving golf legends Bobby Jones, Walter Hagen, and hometown ace Rannulph Junuh. As a teenager, Junuh (played by Matt Damon) had tremendous promise as a golfer. But after his World War I tour of duty, he is marred psychologically and loses interest in golf. Content to gamble and drink, Junuh is a recluse until his former girlfriend invites him to join Jones and Hagen in an exhibition match. Throughout the movie, Junuh seeks to find purpose in his life, although he is fearful of what that purpose might be.

During the exhibition match, with four holes to play in the final round, Junuh successfully overcomes his several strokes deficit and takes a two-stroke lead. But by the sixteenth hole, he trails again. On the seventeenth hole, he slices his tee shot deep into the woods. As he enters the dark forest to find his ball, panic overtakes him. The steam evaporating from the ground triggers memories of smoking battlefields where he watched all his company die. His hands tremble, and he drops his clubs. Once he finds his ball, he calls it quits. He remembers why he quit playing golf and started drinking. Just then,

Bagger, his golfing mentor (played by Will Smith), finds him and asks which club he'd like from his bag. He proceeds to tell Junuh that his problems have to do with the grip the past holds on him.

"Ain't a soul on this entire earth ain't got a burden to carry he can't understand," Bagger consoles. "You ain't alone in that. But you've been carrying this one long enough. It's time to lay it down."

Junuh admits, "I don't know how!"

Bagger replies, "You got a choice. You can stop, or you can start walking right back to where you've been and just stand there. It's time for you to come out of the shadows, Junuh! It's time for you to choose!"

"I can't," Junuh protests.

"Yes, you can," Bagger counters. "You're not alone. I'm right here with you. I've been here all along. Now play the game. Your game. The only one you were meant to play. The one that was given to you when you came into this world. Now's the time!"

Elapsed time: Measured from the beginning of the opening credit, this scene begins at 01:36:50 and lasts approximately four and one-half minutes.

Content: Rated PG-13 for profanity and vulgarity

Citation: *The Legend of Bagger Vance* (DreamWorks, 2000), written by Jeremy Leven (based on a novel by Steven Pressfield), directed by Robert Redford

submitted by Greg Asimakoupoulos, Naperville, Illinois

50. HUMAN WORTH

Schindler's List

Topic: *People Rather Than Gold*

Texts: *Matthew 16:26; Matthew 28:19–20; Mark 8:35–37; 1 Corinthians 9:22; 1 Corinthians 10:33*

Keywords: *Courage; Evangelism; Giving; Human Worth; Ministry; Missions; Money; Possessions; Sacrifice; Values*

The award-winning film *Schindler's List* tells the story of how Oskar Schindler (played by Liam Neeson), a German entrepreneur, first exploits but later protects Jews in Poland. When Jews are forced into the ghetto, Schindler employs them at his kitchenware factory. This arrangement is beneficial for both Schindler, who gets cheap labor, and the Jews, who are protected from being sent to concentration camps. When the Nazis close Poland's Krakow ghetto, Jews are either sent to death camps or a labor camp at Plaszow. At Plaszow, many workers die, and those who are not productive are transferred to nearby Auschwitz.

When the tide turns on the Eastern Front and the German forces retreat, Schindler begins manufacturing faulty artillery for the German army. Disillusioned with the Nazi party, Schindler conspires with his Jewish accountant, Itzhak Stern (played by Ben Kingsley), to employ Jews from Plaszow, hence saving them from extermination.

When Germany finally surrenders, Schindler knows he is a wanted man for wrongly using Jews as slave labor. As he prepares to flee, Schindler is surrounded by over a thousand Jews whose lives he saved. His accountant-turned-friend, Itzhak, hands Schindler a piece of paper and says, "We've written a letter trying to explain things in case you were captured. Every worker has signed it."

Schindler is moved by this gesture and thanks them. Itzhak then gives Schindler a gold ring with an inscription on it, which Itzhak translates: "It's Hebrew from the Talmud. It says, 'Whoever saves one life saves the entire world.'"

Weeping, Schindler cries out, "I could have got more! I could have got more!"

Itzhak reassures him, "Eleven hundred people are alive because of you."

Schindler laments, "If I made more money—I threw away so much money. You have no idea. If I just . . ."

Again, Itzhak emphasizes that Schindler has saved generations because of what he did.

"I didn't do enough," Schindler says.

"You did so much," Itzhak reaffirms.

Emotionally undone, Schindler muses, "This car—what use is this car? Why did I keep this car? I could have saved ten more people." Then taking off his Nazi lapel badge, he guiltily says, "This is gold; I could have saved more."

The film tells us that today there are more than six thousand descendants of Schindler's Jews living in the United States and Europe, as well as many in Israel.

All the world's possessions are not as precious as one person.

Elapsed time: Measured from the beginning of the opening credit, this scene begins at 02:40:00 and lasts approximately five minutes.

Content: Rated R for nudity, violence, and profanity

Citation: *Schindler's List* (Universal, 1993), written by Steve Zaillian (based on the novel by Thomas Keneally), directed by Steven Spielberg

submitted by David Holdaway, Aberdeen, Scotland

51. INJUSTICE

Glory

Topic: *Standing with the Oppressed*

Texts: *2 Chronicles 19:6–7; Amos 5:15; Romans 12:9–10; 2 Corinthians 8:9; Philippians 1:27*

Keywords: *Brotherhood; Brotherly Love; Community; Convictions; Courage; Injustice; Justice; Leadership; Racism; Sacrifice; Unity*

The movie *Glory* chronicles the true story of the first noncommissioned black regiment to fight for the North during the Civil War. The formation of the 54th Regiment of Massachusetts is not taken seriously from the beginning. Most doubt that enough soldiers will volunteer. Others suspect that even if enough did enlist, the regiment would whittle away, deserter by deserter. But the white abolitionist officer from Boston, Robert Shaw (played by Matthew Broderick), idealistically agrees to command the 54th, believing that blacks should be given the right to fight for their freedom.

From the beginning, Shaw tries to treat his men like soldiers, not like the slaves they once were. Even though the Union doesn't consider the 54th equal in status with other white regiments, Shaw wants his soldiers equipped as every other soldier is in the North—with firmly soled shoes, Union uniforms, and sturdy weaponry. Lobbying on behalf of his regiment, however, he increasingly understands how little his men are valued, even by those Northerners who maintain that blacks should be emancipated.

Throughout the film Shaw faces the dilemma of standing up for his men or staying quiet among his superiors in order to save face. This dilemma is strikingly portrayed when Shaw must inform his soldiers that the Union recently determined that black soldiers would receive a smaller salary than white soldiers. Standing on a high, commanding platform, Shaw hesitantly announces to his troops, "You men enlisted in this regiment with the understanding that you would be paid the regular army wage of thirteen dollars a month. This morning I have been notified that, since you are a colored regiment, you will be paid ten dollars a month."

His regiment grumbles at the injustice, but they fall out by company to receive their pay. Even a little pay is better than no pay at all. But there is one dissenter, a runaway slave named Trip (played by Denzel Washington), who stridently protests the pay cut.

"Where you goin', boy?" Trip asks one soldier.

"To get paid. Ten dollar, lot of money," his comrade replies.

Trying to garner some support, Trip asks his elderly bunk mate, Rawlins (played by Morgan Freeman), "Hey pop, are you gonna lay down for this too?"

When Rawlins ignores him, Trip files up and down the forming lines, struggling to get someone to join his protest. He hollers, "A colored soldier will stop a bullet just as good as a white one and for less money too. Yeah, yeah, Ol' Unc' Abe has got himself a real bargain here."

Soon other soldiers join the protest. One yells, "That's right, slaves. Step right up. Make your mark. Get your slave wage." Another says, "All you good colored boys, go ahead and sign up."

One by one, soldiers join the outcry, and Trip incites the regiment to tear up their paychecks. "Tear it up. Tear it up. Tear it up," he shouts.

The regiment repeats the same words: "Tear it up. Tear it up. Tear it up."

"Pow!" A shot instantly silences the clamor. The soldiers turn their attention to their commanding officer, Robert Shaw, expecting to be disciplined.

"If you men will take no pay," Shaw sternly announces, "then none of us will." He proceeds to tear up his check as well.

Recovering from their shock, the soldiers uproariously celebrate, tossing their tattered paychecks into the air like confetti.

Elapsed time: Measured from the initial studio logo, this scene begins at 00:53:35 and lasts two minutes and forty-five seconds.

Content: Rated R for graphic violence and some profanity

Citation: *Glory* (Tri-Star Pictures, 1989), written by Kevin Jarre (based in part on the letters of the real Colonel Shaw), directed by Edward Zwick

submitted by Melissa Parks, Des Plaines, Illinois

The Devil's Own

Topic: *Integrity Tested*

Texts: *Exodus 20:16; Psalm 15:2–5; Psalm 38:18; Ephesians 4:25; 1 Timothy 1:5; 1 Timothy 1:19*

Keywords: *Career; Character; Choices; Compromise; Conscience; Guilt; Honesty; Integrity; Lying; Work*

In the movie *The Devil's Own,* Harrison Ford plays an ethical New York City cop named Tom O'Meara. Almost halfway through the film, Tom and his partner, Eddie (played by Ruben Blades), chase a teenager caught trying to steal a car radio. The thief shoots at them twice and then throws away the gun. Tom stops to retrieve the gun while Eddie runs past him. Suddenly, Tom hears a shot. Moments later, standing over the lifeless body of the teenager, Tom says to his partner, "He's dead, man. Half his face is gone. What happened?"

Eddie explains, "He was getting away. And then he turned around with the gun in his hand."

Tom yells, "You shot him in the back, Eddie! Here's his gun. He tossed it around the corner."

Eddie desperately looks around him. He takes the gun from Tom and drops it beside the body. As they look at each other, Eddie's eyes plead with Tom to cover for him. Tom turns around and walks away as Eddie helplessly shouts, "He shot at us, Tommy! He shot at us!"

Later at the precinct, when they both are questioned about the shooting, Tom lies to cover for his partner, Eddie.

Later, guilt-ridden, Tom talks about the shooting with his wife (played by Margaret Colin): "Sheila, that Lopez guy didn't have a gun in his hand when he was shot. He tossed it. It was nuts out there. [Eddie] didn't see him toss it. I had the gun in my hand when Eddie shot him. It was a bad call."

His wife responds, "Well, you covered for him."

Tom insists, "I lied about how it went down. I thought it through, Sheila. I'm going to take my pension—retire."

"Twenty-three years and you never took a bribe. You never abused your power. You never treated anyone unfairly," Sheila says.

"I treated the dead guy unfair," Tom says.

"He shot at you," she argues.

Tom says, "He was stealing radios. He got shot in the back. You don't deserve to get killed for stealing a radio."

Sheila says, "Tom, it's terrible that he died. But you're not the only cop on the force who's made a mistake. Besides, you didn't make the mistake. *Eddie* did!"

Tom yells, "I lied! Don't you understand? There are some things I said I would never do."

"Once, Tom. You did it once."

"What about next time?" Tom asks. "I can't do the job this way. I'm done being a cop."

"But you love being a cop," his wife says.

Tom pauses and responds, "I love you. I love the kids. I love what we got. I don't love being a cop—anymore."

Elapsed time: Measured from the beginning of the opening credit, the first scene begins at 00:51:50 and ends at 00:54:26. The second scene begins at 01:00:00 and ends at 01:02:00.

Content: Rated R for violence, profanity, and nudity

Citation: *The Devil's Own* (Columbia Pictures, 1997), written by Kevin Jarre, David A. Cohen, and Vincent Patrick, directed by Alan J. Pakula

submitted by Jerry De Luca, Montreal West,
Quebec, Canada

53. INTEGRITY

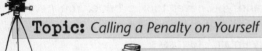

The Legend of Bagger Vance

Topic: *Calling a Penalty on Yourself*

Texts: *Genesis 3:1–5; Proverbs 10:9; Matthew 4:1–11; Luke 4:1–13*

Keywords: *Confession; Courage; Honesty; Integrity; Sin; Temptation; Truth*

The Legend of Bagger Vance is a movie about a mythical golf match set in the 1930s in Savannah, Georgia, involving golf legends Bobby Jones, Walter Hagen, and hometown ace Rannulph Junuh. As a teenager, Junuh (played by Matt Damon) had Tiger Woods-level promise. But after his World War I tour of duty, he is marred psychologically and loses interest in golf. Content to gamble and drink, Junuh is a recluse until his former girlfriend invites him to join Jones and Hagen in an exhibition match.

Junuh, encouraged by a community that recalls his prewar glory, reluctantly agrees to participate. While hitting practice balls in his backyard, Junuh meets a transient by the name of Bagger Vance (played by Will Smith). Vance offers to caddie for Junuh in the upcoming match and is determined to help him rediscover his passion for the game.

On the final hole of the seventy-two-hole competition, all three golfers are tied. Junuh hits his tee shot into a wooded area. He walks into the woods with Bagger and Hardy, Junuh's ten-year-old junior caddy (played by J. Michael Moncrief), and examines the difficulty of his lie. While moving some twigs and leaves that would impede his shot, his ball moves (which in golf is an automatic one-stroke penalty).

"The ball moved!" Junuh exclaims. "I have to call a penalty on myself."

Hardy, who is desperate for his hero to win, cries out, "No! No! Don't do it, please. Only you and me seen it, and I won't tell a soul. Cross my heart. No one will know."

"I will, Hardy," Junuh says, "and so will you!"

Hardy pleads to Bagger. "You gotta tell him not to do it, Bagger. It's just a stupid rule that doesn't mean nothing."

Bagger responds, "That's a choice for Mr. Junuh, Hardy."

While Junuh determines what to do, onlookers tempt him to lie. "Maybe the ball moved before you touched the twigs," suggests one of Junuh's supporters. "The light plays funny tricks on your eyes," pleads another. Even the referee tries to convince the young player that his guilt is misplaced.

But Junuh confesses and continues his game with integrity. Then he steps up to the ball and hits it within several feet of the hole.

Elapsed time: Measured from the beginning of the opening credit, this scene begins at 01:45:47 and lasts approximately two minutes.

Content: Rated PG-13 for mild profanity and sensuality

Citation: *The Legend of Bagger Vance* (DreamWorks, 2000), written by Jeremy Leven (based on a novel by Steven Pressfield), directed by Robert Redford

submitted by Greg Asimakoupoulos, Naperville, Illinois

54. JEALOUSY

Amadeus

Topic: *Danger of Selfish Ambition*

Texts: *Matthew 16:26; Romans 13:13; 1 Corinthians 3:3; Galatians 5:19–21; 2 Timothy 3:8; Hebrews 6:6; Hebrews 10:26–27; Hebrews 12:25*

Keywords: *Ambition; Betrayal; Envy; Hardness of Heart; Jealousy; Pride; Selfishness; Sin; Vanity*

The winner of eight Academy Awards, *Amadeus* is a fascinating study of the way in which jealousy destroys those who cannot accept the fact that God sometimes gives remarkable gifts to undeserving people. This fictional story explores the competitive relationship between Antonio Salieri (played by F. Murray Abraham), a gifted classical musician, and Wolfgang Amadeus Mozart (played by Tom Hulce), an even greater musician who continually outshines Salieri. Salieri, court composer to the eighteenth-century Austrian emperor, knew from childhood that he was destined to write music, and he dreamed of becoming great. Recognizing that music was from God, he bargained with the Almighty:

Lord, make me a great composer. Let me celebrate your glory through music and be celebrated myself. Make me famous throughout the world, dear God. Make me immortal. After I die, let people speak my name forever with love for what I wrote. In return, I will give you my chastity, my industry, my deepest humility, every hour of my life.

Although Salieri becomes a well-respected musician, he knows nothing of the fame or talent God gives Mozart.

In the movie, Mozart is depicted as profligate, spending more money than he makes. When in dire financial straits, Mozart's young bride, Constanze, requests Salieri to help her sell some of her husband's manuscripts. As Salieri reads each manuscript, he plays the notes in his head, astonished by the perfection of each composition. Wildly jealous, he exits the room and sits in his parlor, contemplating why God allowed Mozart to drink of the fame for which he's thirsted all his life. Angered, he pulls the crucifix off the wall and throws it into the blazing fireplace.

He speaks the following words to God:

From now on we are enemies, you and I. Because you choose for your instrument a boastful, lustful, smutty, infantile boy and give me for my reward only the ability to recognize the incarnation; because you are unjust, unfair, unkind, I will block you. I swear it. I will hinder and harm your creature on earth. As far as I am able, I will ruin your incarnation.

Elapsed time: Measured from the beginning of the opening credit, this scene begins at 00:57:20 and lasts approximately one minute.

Content: Rated PG for profanity and vulgarity

Citation: *Amadeus* (Orion, 1984), written by Peter Shaffer, directed by Milos Forman

submitted by Greg Asimakoupoulos, Naperville, Illinois

55. KINDNESS

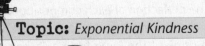

Pay It Forward

Topic: *Exponential Kindness*

Texts: *Luke 10:30–37; Galatians 5:22–23; Colossians 3:12*

Keywords: *Generosity; Giving; Kindness; Love; Ministry; Servanthood*

Pay It Forward is a movie about a seventh grader's ingenious plan to make a difference in the world. On the first day of school, Trevor McKinney (played by Haley Joel Osment) and his classmates are challenged by their social studies teacher, Mr. Simonet (played by Kevin Spacey), to change the world. Written on the blackboard, the challenge reads: "Think of an idea to change our world—and put it into action." While most children disinterestedly slouch in their desks, Trevor is mesmerized by the possibility of changing the world.

As Trevor rides his dirt bike back to the modest home in which he and his struggling alcoholic mom live, he detours to a place where the homeless gather. An unkempt, unshaven man devouring a chocolate cookie catches Trevor's eye. Motivated by his teacher's challenge, Trevor invites the man to come and sleep in his garage. Trevor's mother (played by Helen Hunt) is unaware of this arrangement until she awakens one evening to find the homeless man working on her broken-down pickup. Holding the man at gunpoint, she asks him to explain himself. He starts the truck to show her that he has successfully repaired it and tells her about Trevor's kindness. He says, "Somebody comes along like your son and gives me a leg up, I'll take it. I can't mess up again, or I'll be dead. I'm just paying it forward."

Quizzically, Trevor's mom asks, "What's paying it forward?"

The next day Trevor explains to his class his amazing plan of paying it forward. Mr. Simonet and Trevor's classmates are enthralled by Trevor's idea. To explain his plan, he draws a circle and explains, "That's me." Underneath it, he draws three other circles, saying, "That's three other people. I'm going to help them, but it has to be something really big—something they can't do for themselves. So I do it for them, and they do it for three people. That's nine people." And nine lives turn into twenty-seven.

As the movie proceeds, "paying it forward" changes the lives of the rich, the poor, the homeless, and a prisoner.

Elapsed time: Measured from the beginning of the opening credit, the garage scene begins at 00:30:16 and ends at 00:33:51.

Content: Rated PG-13 for vulgarity and profanity

Citation: *Pay It Forward* (Warner Brothers, 2000), written by Leslie Dixon (based on the novel *Pay It Forward* by Catherine Ryan Hyde), directed by Mimi Leder

submitted by David Slagle, Lawrenceville, Georgia

Sandy Bottom Orchestra

Topic: *Loving Your Enemies*

Texts: *Luke 6:35–37; Acts 2:42–47; Romans 12:13; Ephesians 4:28; Colossians 3:13; Hebrews 13:16; James 1:27; 1 John 3:17*

Keywords: *Church; Community; Enemies; Forgiveness; Grace; Human Help; Kindness; Love; Mercy; Unconditional Love*

Sandy Bottom Orchestra is a poignant story (based on a novel by American humorist Garrison Keillor and his wife, Jenny Lind Nilsson) that illustrates how compassion heals bitter self-righteousness. This made-for-TV movie revolves around a rural community in northern Wisconsin—Sandy Bottom. Although Sandy Bottom is comprised of good people, the community is ignorant of cultural arts. This poses a particular frustration to Norman and Ingrid Green (played by Tom Irwin and Glenne Headley), who move to Sandy Bottom from Minneapolis. Norman operates the local dairy, and Ingrid is Bethesda Lutheran Church's choir director. While preparing for a classical concert for the annual Dairy Days festival, the people of Sandy Bottom struggle to accept one another's differences.

Because Ingrid has a harsh attitude, Pastor Sykes (played by Richard McMillan) fires her. Without a paying job she pours herself into a campaign to save a historic old building the mayor is committed to tear down. At a campaign rally she discovers that Pastor Sykes's wife is hospitalized in Minneapolis for severe clinical depression, leaving her husband to care for their three sons. Despite her anger about losing her job, Ingrid is deeply troubled by the minister's plight. She slaves away in the kitchen and secretly deposits a week's worth of food at the Sykes's front door. Unbeknownst to her, he sees her unanticipated act of kindness.

In church the next day the choir opens the service singing a familiar old hymn, but its unpolished performance proves they are without a director. Reverend Sykes approaches the pulpit and speaks.

"Good morning. Before we begin today, I would like to take a moment to thank you all for your concern about Miriam. I have communicated your cards and your calls to her, and I believe they are helping."

He struggles to find the right words and abashedly looks at the floor before beginning again. "I'd like to tell you about one generous act in particular that has surprised me. I thought, having ministered for fifteen years, there were no more surprises. But I was wrong. Last night somebody left a week's worth of meals for me and my boys on our front porch. There was no note, just the reassurance in that lovely act of kindness that we are not alone. In my deep distress I had come to believe we were. How wrong I was. We misjudge each other if, in the heat of argument or disagreement or in the simple routines of daily life, we fail to see that God is in each of us always—struggling to love and to be loved in return. We are none of us alone. We belong to each other."

Eyeing Ingrid in the congregation, he adds, "I thank you, my anonymous friend, for refreshing my faith."

Elapsed time: Measured from the opening credit, this scene begins at 00:54:33 and lasts approximately five minutes.

Content: Rated G

Citation: *Sandy Bottom Orchestra* (Showtime, 2000), written by Joseph Maurer (based on the novel *Sandy Bottom Orchestra* by Garrison Keillor and Jenny Lind Nilsson), directed by Bradley Wigor

submitted by Greg Asimakoupoulos, Naperville, Illinois

57. LEADERSHIP

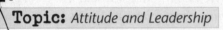

Remember the Titans

Topic: *Attitude and Leadership*

Texts: *Matthew 20:25–28; John 13:1–17;*
1 Corinthians 4:16; 1 Corinthians 11:1;
Philippians 4:2; 1 Thessalonians 1:5–6;
Hebrews 10:24

Keywords: *Attitude; Communication; Community; Conflict; Confrontation; Cooperation; Friendship; Leadership; Racism; Reconciliation; Relationships; Sacrifice; Selfishness; Sports; Teamwork; Unity*

Based on a true story, *Remember the Titans* spotlights the character formation of those caught up in the difficult transition of integrating T. C. Williams High School in Alexandria, Virginia. In 1971 the tensions run high—especially on the football team—when a black man, Herman Boone (played by Denzel Washington), is brought in as the new head coach, demoting the previously successful white coach, Bill Yoast (played by Will Patton), to an assistant position.

About thirty minutes into the movie, the team is at the breaking point. It's been rife with tension, bickering, and racial struggles. In fact, it's not much of a team at all. This scene is the turning point, as team captain and All-American linebacker Gary Bertier (played by Ryan Hurst), who is white, has a confrontation with the other key defensive leader, Julius Campbell (played by Wood Harris), who is black. They've been forced by Coach Boone to talk to each other, which neither one of them likes at all, but at last they get down to the issues at the root of the problem—attitude and leadership.

Gary and Julius stand nose to nose, and every line is heated.

Julius says, "Why should I give a hoot about you, huh? Or anybody else out there? . . . You're the captain right?"

"Right," says Gary.

"You have a job?" asks Julius.

"I have a job," says Gary.

Julius asks, "You been doin' your job?"

Gary says, "I've been doin' my job."

Julius says, "The captain is supposed to be a leader. Then why don't you tell your white buddies to block for Rev [the black running back] better, because they haven't blocked for him worth a plugged nickel, and you know it. Nobody plays, yourself included. . . . I'm supposed to wear myself out for the team? What team? No! No, what I'm gonna do is I'm gonna look out for myself, and I'm gonna get mine!"

Gary says, "That's the worst attitude I ever heard."

Julius answers, "Attitude reflects leadership."

In the next practice, the moment of truth arrives. Gary stands up to his white friends and tells them to block for Rev, and they actually follow his lead. Soon after, he and Julius are working together tightly on defense, and the next thing you know, they are slapping heads together like they won the Super Bowl, flush with a new and growing respect and friendship. The team follows their lead and becomes incredibly united, eventually leading the school and even the community through the process of racial integration.

If we are leaders, those around us know whether we are out for ourselves or out for the team, and their attitudes will reflect it.

Elapsed time: This scene lasts two minutes and begins at 00:28:45, measured from the beginning of the opening scene.

Content: Rated PG for thematic elements and mild profanity

Citation: *Remember the Titans* (Disney, 2000), written by Gregory Allen Howard, directed by Boaz Yakin

submitted by Bill White, Paramount, California

58. LEADERSHIP

U-571

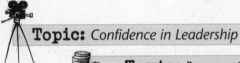

Topic: *Confidence in Leadership*

Texts: *Romans 12:8; 1 Corinthians 2:1–5; 1 Peter 5:3*

Keywords: *Attitudes and Emotions; Confidence; Humility; Leadership; Leadership of the Church; Ministry; Rebuke; Trust*

In the movie *U–571*, actor Matthew McConaughey plays Lieutenant Andrew Tyler, a World War II naval officer assigned to a United States submarine on a mission to capture a secret Nazi code from a damaged U-boat. During the mission, Tyler's sub is sunk, and the captain is killed. Tyler, now thrust into command, commandeers the Nazi U-boat with his remaining crew.

As they gather inside the U-boat, the Americans realize how desperate their situation is. They know they can't radio for help because the Germans will likely intercept the message, realize that the code has been compromised, and move to change it. The crew looks to Tyler, who says, "Do you think I have all the answers? Do you think I know how we're going to get out of this mess? I don't. I don't know how."

Later, Tyler is sitting alone when he is joined by Chief Klough (played by Harvey Keitel). Tyler reminisces about how he used to work on his father's rusty, noisy fishing boat. He vowed that he would never skipper a boat like that. Instead, he saw himself on the bridge of a battleship, being "a real sea captain."

When given permission to speak freely, Chief Klough says to Tyler, "This is the Navy, where a commanding officer's a mighty and terrible thing—a man to be feared and respected. All-knowing, all-powerful. Don't you dare say what you said to the boys back there again—'I don't know.' Those three words will kill a crew, dead as a depth charge. You're the skipper now, and the skipper always knows what to do, whether he does or not."

Any Christian in leadership knows the tension portrayed in this movie. People look to us as the "all-knowing and all-powerful skipper," and we feel the need to at least create the illusion that we know what to do, even if we don't. To show weakness and uncertainty (we think) kills the confidence of the people we lead.

Elapsed time: This scene begins at 01:02:57 and goes to 01:04:42.

Content: Rated PG-13 for war violence and occasional profanity

Citation: *U–571* (Universal, 2000), written by Jonathan Mostow, Sam Montgomery, and David Ayer, directed by Jonathan Mostow

submitted by Stephen Nordbye, Charlton, Massachusetts

Addicted to Love

Topic: *The Object of Our Creator's Affection*

Texts: *2 Chronicles 16:9; Ephesians 5:25–32; 1 John 3:1*

Keywords: *Affection; Christ's Love; God's Love; Human Love; Relationships; Romance; Romantic Love*

Addicted to Love tells the story of a small-town astronomer by the name of Sam (played by Matthew Broderick) whose love for his girlfriend, Linda (played by Kelly Preston), is deeply tested. Sam's romantic love for Linda is illustrated early in the movie as we find him at work at the observatory.

He has his telescope trained on a star that is in the process of turning into a supernova. The amazing discovery is an obvious source of excitement for a visiting scientist. As the clock approaches high noon, one of Sam's colleagues calls his attention to the time. Without explanation Sam turns the telescope away from the heavens and aims it at a school playground. The visiting scientist can't believe that the clock—or anything else on earth—could be so important as to suspend the once-in-a-lifetime look at a supernova being born. Carl, one of Sam's associates, tries to explain.

"Professor, there's this other phenomenon that Sam gives his priority to every morning," Carl says.

The guest scientist asks, "What could be more important?"

Sam, without skipping a beat, aims the telescope at a school playground several miles away. Through the telescope he sees Linda.

In the midst of her responsibilities as a schoolteacher, she glances at her watch and then proceeds to look in the direction of the observatory. In what has become a practiced ritual, Linda smiles and waves.

Elapsed time: Measured from the beginning of the opening credit, this scene begins at 00:00:45 and lasts about one and one-half minutes.

Content: Rated R for language and sexual situations

Citation: *Addicted to Love* (Warner Brothers, 1997), written by Robert Gordon, directed by Griffin Dunne

submitted by Greg Asimakoupoulos, Naperville, Illinois, and Doug Scott, Elgin, Illinois

60. LOVE

The Hurricane

Topic: *Love Sets Us Free*

Texts: *John 3:16–21; Ephesians 2:1–6;*
Philippians 4:10–19; Philemon 1;
Hebrews 13:3

Keywords: *Adversity; Bondage; Despair; Freedom;*
Friendship; Gratitude; Human Help; Injustice; Justice;
Love; Loyalty; Oppression; Prisons; Racism; Redemption;
Relationships; Rescue; Youth

Denzel Washington stars in *The Hurricane,* the true story of professional boxer Rubin "Hurricane" Carter's life. At the height of his boxing career in the 1960s, Carter is falsely accused of murder by a racist police force and sentenced to prison for the remainder of his natural life.

While Carter is in prison, a young black boy, Lesra, who has read Carter's autobiography, befriends Hurricane. Their friendship deepens over time, and the boy introduces Carter to a few of his adult friends, who become convinced of his innocence and commit themselves to helping as his amateur lawyers and detectives. After some twenty years in lockup, Carter, fifty years old, is granted a new trial. While awaiting the verdict in his prison cell, Carter and Lesra share their thoughts.

Carter says, "We've come a long way, huh, little brother?"

Lesra nods in agreement, pauses, and then boasts, "Rubin, I just want you to know—if this doesn't work, I'm bustin' you outta here."

"You are, huh?" responds Carter.

"Yeah, that's right, I'm bustin' you outta here," insists Lesra.

After a moment of silence, Carter changes the subject and states his belief that they were not brought together by chance.

Carter pauses and then emphatically continues, "Hate put me in prison. Love's gonna bust me out."

Lesra responds, "Just in case love doesn't, I'm gonna bust you outta here."

Carter laughs. He reaches out to touch Lesra's face and wipe away a tear. Clenching Lesra's hand, Carter responds in a hushed tone, "You already have, Lesra."

Elapsed time: Measured from the beginning of the opening credit, this scene begins at 02:17:32 and lasts approximately two minutes.

Content: Rated R for some profanity and brief but extreme violence

Citation: *The Hurricane* (Universal Pictures and Beacon Pictures, 1999), written by Armyan Bernstein and Dan Gordon (based on *The Sixteenth Round* by Rubin Carter and *Lazarus and the Hurricane* by Sam Chaiton and Terry Swinton), directed by Norman Jewison

submitted by Elaine Larson, Barrington, Illinois

61. LOVE

Tuesdays with Morrie

Topic: *We Need Love to Live*

Texts: *Genesis 2:18; Matthew 22:37–40; John 13:34–35; John 15:9–12; 1 Corinthians 13; 1 John 4:7–8*

Keywords: *Community; Love; Meaning of Life; Mentoring; Self-Sufficiency; Service; Wisdom*

The 1999 movie *Tuesdays with Morrie,* based on the book by the same name, is the true story of a sportswriter, Mitch Albom, and his reunion with his former college professor, who is dying of amyotrophic lateral sclerosis (ALS). Albom (played by Hank Azaria) was a multitasking workaholic, whose life was a series of hurried appointments, rushed phone calls, and last-minute sprints to catch a flight. When he discovers that his former college professor and friend, Morrie Schwartz (played by Jack Lemmon), is in the last stages of ALS, he honors a long-overdue promise to visit.

In these visits, Morrie teaches Mitch important lessons about what matters most in life. Morrie is sometimes patient with Mitch's superficiality, but in the following scene Morrie confronts Mitch with some painful truths.

Morrie is very frail and is lying in a recliner in obvious pain. He grimaces and asks Mitch to rub his aching feet with salve. "When we're infants," says Morrie, "we need people to survive; when we're dying, we need people to survive—but here's the secret: In between, we need each other even more."

Mitch nods and responds with a quote he's heard Morrie say many times: "We must love one another or die."

Morrie loses patience with Mitch. "Yeah, but do you believe that? Does it apply to you?"

Mitch is stunned and defensive as he confesses that he doesn't know what he believes. The world he lives in doesn't allow for the contemplation of spiritual things.

Morrie pushes a little harder. "You hate that word, don't you—*spiritual?* You think it's just touchy-feely stuff, huh?"

"I just don't understand it," says Mitch.

"We must love one another or die," says Morrie. "It's a very simple lesson, Mitch."

Elapsed time: This scene begins at 01:10:54 and goes to 01:12:24.

Content: Rated PG for profanity

Citation: *Tuesdays with Morrie* (Touchstone, 1999), written by Thomas Rickman (based on the book *Tuesdays with Morrie* by Mitch Albom), directed by Mick Jackson

submitted by David Slagle, Lawrenceville, Georgia

62. MARRIAGE

Family Man

Topic: *Choosing Us Versus Me*

Texts: *1 Corinthians 13:4–7; Ephesians 5:21–33*

Keywords: *Family; Husbands; Love; Marriage; Selfishness; Self-Sacrifice; Self-Sufficiency; Wives*

In the movie *Family Man,* Jack Campbell (played by Nicolas Cage) is the successful president of an investment house in New York City—and he's happily single. He has everything, or so he thinks, including a sports car and a radiant girlfriend. But on Christmas morning his world turns upside down. He wakes up in a "what if?" scenario, finding himself twelve years into marriage with his college sweetheart and two small children. He desperately tries to rediscover his old life but in the process begins to find out what he's really been missing all these years. In particular, he finds that living life for yourself alone is not as fulfilling as living your life for others.

Toward the end of the movie, Jack discusses with his wife a job opportunity that would revive some of his former glory. Taking the job would mean a big move for the family, but Kate (played by Téa Leoni) says she's willing to make a sacrifice for the sake of the family—a defining moment that helps Jack see what marriage is all about. Kate makes this declaration: "Maybe I was being naive, but I believed that we would grow old together in this house. That we'd spend holidays here and have our grandchildren come visit us here. I had this image of us all gray and wrinkly and me working in the garden and you repainting the deck. Things change. If you need this, Jack, if you really need this—I'll take these kids from the life they love, and I'll take myself from the only home we've ever known together, and I'll move wherever you need to go. I'll do that because I love you. I love you. And that's more important to me than our address. I choose us."

Elapsed time: Measured from the beginning of the opening credit, this scene begins at 01:34:00 and lasts less than two minutes.

Content: Rated PG-13 for sensuality and some profanity

Citation: *The Family Man* (Universal Pictures, 2000), written by David Diamond and David Weissman, directed by Brett Ratner

submitted by Bill White, Paramount, California

63. MARRIAGE

Father of the Bride

Topic: *Daddy Remembers to Love Wife*

Texts: *Proverbs 5:18–19; Ephesians 5:25–33*

Keywords: *Attitudes and Emotions; Husbands; Love; Marriage; Men; Parents; Romance; Weddings*

Father of the Bride is a touching comedy-drama dealing with a father's feelings about giving his daughter away in marriage. George, the father (played by Steve Martin), narrates the story in flashback fashion and focuses heavily on pleasing his daughter, (played by Kimberly Williams) even to the point of hiring a wedding planner and agreeing to having the reception—with hundreds of guests—held in his own home.

A critical plot question is, *Will George focus so heavily on his daughter and her happiness that his wife will become lost in the shuffle?* After all, he's not just the "father of the bride"; he is still a husband.

Toward the end of the film, the day of the wedding has finally arrived—and things couldn't be going worse. For one thing, there is snow, lots of it—in southern California, no less! The wedding planners are caught up in shoveling rather than organizing the reception. The florist is trying desperately to thaw out the freshly planted walkway tulips—with a hair dryer. The swans that were supposed to be floating gracefully in a newly built fountain pool are instead warming themselves in the porcelain tub of an upstairs bathroom!

All of this for George's beloved daughter.

But what about his wife, Nina (played by Diane Keaton)? Has she been forgotten? It appears so, until one poignant scene. George stands at the front door, in a hurry to be on time for the ceremony in the garden. He glances up. There at the top of the stairs is Nina, his wife of many years, smiling down at him. "All right," she says. "Relax, honey. Everything's going to be just fine. At least we know they can't start without us." Nina is radiant, gorgeous. And at that moment George recalls that he, too, still has a bride on this day.

He looks at her again—and sees beauty. We hear him thinking, *I knew I'd never be able to remember what Nina wore that day. But I also knew I'd never forget the way she looked.*

He hugs and kisses her. "Nina," he says, "you shouldn't look this beautiful. It's not fair to the bride."

Elapsed time: Measured from the initial flashing of the studio symbol, this scene begins at 01:20:50 and ends at 01:24:00.

Content: Rated PG—generally morally acceptable, reinforcing the values of fidelity, family, and a high view of marriage; there are, however, a few instances of mildly offensive language and a scene of drinking in a bar.

Citation: *Father of the Bride* (Touchstone Pictures, 1991, a remake of the 1950 film), written by Nancy Meyers and Charles Shyer (from the 1950 screenplay by Francis Goodrich and Albert Hackett, based on the novel by Edward Streeter), directed by Charles Shyer

submitted by Gary Wilde

64. MENTORING

Finding Forrester

Topic: *Two-Way Mentoring*

Texts: *2 Kings 2:1–14; Proverbs 27:17;*
Romans 1:11–12; 2 Timothy 2:2;
Philemon 1

Keywords: *Community; Discipleship; Fear; Friendship;*
Growth; Learning; Loneliness; Mentoring; Relationships;
Spiritual Formation; Spiritual Growth; Teenagers; Youth

Finding Forrester, starring Sean Connery as Forrester, is about a reclusive writer who, after winning the Pulitzer Prize for his first novel, locks himself inside his apartment to hide from the world. Forrester lives off the royalties generated by his classic novel and spends his time reading and writing an occasional article. He refuses to write another book. From his window, Forrester uses binoculars to watch the world outside. To the kids playing ball in the playground below, Forrester is known simply as "The Window."

On a dare, a high school student, Jamal (played by Robert Brown), breaks into Forrester's apartment. Jamal is frightened by Forrester and runs off, leaving his backpack behind. Forrester opens the pack and discovers that Jamal is a budding writer. Forrester edits several of Jamal's writing journals and later throws the backpack containing the journals out the window as Jamal passes below.

These events initiate an unlikely but mutually encouraging relationship. Forrester mentors Jamal, developing him into a writer of such skill that his teachers suspect him of plagiarism. Forrester helps transform Jamal from a person with great potential into a person of accomplishment.

Jamal similarly transforms Forrester. As Forrester helps Jamal progress as a writer, Jamal helps Forrester end his self-imposed exile. Because of Jamal's encouragement, Forrester has the courage to go outside alone, ride his bike again, and even travel to visit his homeland, Scotland, before he dies of cancer. It is largely due to Jamal's friendship that Forrester writes a second novel just before his death.

The final scene shows Jamal reading a letter from Forrester, who has already died. Forrester writes, "While I may have waited until the winter of my life to see the things I have seen this past year, there is no doubt I would have waited too long, had it not been for you."

Forrester spurred Jamal to become an accomplished writer while Jamal spurred Forrester to live his life fully. Mentoring goes both ways. We are designed for relationship, and God grows us through the people who help us and through the people we help.

Elapsed time: Measured from the beginning of the opening credit, the final scene begins at 02:09:12 and ends at 02:10:00.

Content: Rated PG-13 for profanity and mature themes

Citation: *Finding Forrester* (Columbia Pictures, 2000), written by Mike Rich, directed by Gus Van Sant

submitted by Dave Gibson, Idaho Falls, Idaho

65. MERCY

A Christmas Story

Topic: *Mom Shows Mercy to Naughty Son*

Texts: *Luke 1:50; Ephesians 2:4–5; Titus 3:3–5; Hebrews 4:16; 1 Peter 1:18–19*

Keywords: *Children; Christmas; Family; Forgiveness; God's Mercy; God's Wrath; Grace; Mercy; Mothers; Passover; Salvation*

A *Christmas Story* is a movie about the many challenges of a boy named Ralphie. All adults, including Santa Claus, seem to conspire against Ralphie's desire to acquire a Red Ryder BB gun. His father is constantly irritable. And the school bully torments him almost daily.

After one particularly trying day at school, Ralphie runs into the bully while walking home from school. Tired of being teased, Ralphie lets his rage get the best of him; he pummels the bully and bursts out in a string of obscenities.

Unbeknownst to Ralphie, his mother hears his tirade. She walks Ralphie home and sends him to his room. As Ralphie waits fearfully for his dad to come home, he lies in his darkened room, staring at the ceiling with tears streaming down his cheeks. Ralphie anticipates the worst punishment.

Ralphie's mother finds the younger brother, Randy, hiding under the sink, crying. She asks, "Randy, what's the matter? What are you crying for?"

Randy sobs, "Daddy's gonna kill Ralphie!" Even little Randy is terrified of the impending wrath that awaits Ralphie. Mom assures Randy that everything is going to work out, but he continues to whimper. As Mom walks about the kitchen trying to prepare supper, she, too, seems to be fretting about what may come.

Still locked in his room, Ralphie continues pondering his fate: *I heard the car pull up the driveway, and a wave of terror broke over me. He'll know what I said—the awful things I said!*

Hearing his dad's voice, Ralphie walks downstairs to meet his fate. After some small talk, Dad asks, "What happened today?" Ralphie realizes it's all about to come out. He looks at his mother with a pained expression.

Surprisingly, his mother responds, "Nothing much. Ralphie had a fight."

Tension rises as Dad puts down the paper and looks at Ralphie with a stern gaze. "A fight? What kind of fight?"

Mom replies, "Oh, you know how boys are. I gave him a talking to. Oh, I see the Bears are playing the Packers Sunday."

It dawns on Ralphie that he has just experienced a modern-day Passover. The doom of which he was so certain passed over him as his mother poured out mercy. A smile breaks across Ralphie's face, and he beams at his mother. Ralphie says to himself, *I slowly realized that I was not about to be destroyed. From then on, things were different between me and my mother.*

Elapsed time: Measured from the beginning of the opening credit, this scene begins at 01:00:00 and ends at 01:03:20.

Content: Rated PG for profanity

Citation: *A Christmas Story* (MGM, 1983), written by Leigh Brown, Bob Clark, and Jean Shepherd (based on Shepherd's *In God We Trust, All Others Pay Cash*), directed by Bob Clark

submitted by David Slagle, Lawrenceville, Georgia

Les Misérables

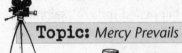

Topic: *Mercy Prevails*

Texts: *Matthew 12:7; Romans 5:12–19;*
Ephesians 2:1–6; James 2:12–13

Keywords: *Enemies; Forgiveness; Freedom; Grace;*
Justice; Law; Mercy

The movie *Les Misérables,* based on Victor Hugo's famous novel, focuses on French investigator Javert's relentless manhunt of a criminal named Jean Valjean (played by Liam Neeson). Valjean goes into hiding to avoid being captured by Javert (played by Geoffrey Rush), who is resolute on returning him to prison. After many years of guarded living, Valjean glimpses freedom when French rebels capture and plan to kill his pursuer. But instead of allowing the rebels to kill Javert, Valjean frees him from the rebels' clutch.

Even after this act of grace, Javert continues to hunt Valjean, determined more than ever to arrest him. Ultimately, Javert discovers Valjean participating in a commoner's revolt against the French establishment. When Valjean spots Javert, he instinctually flees, escaping through the sewage ducts. Javert trudges after him, cornering Valjean at the banks of the Seine River.

Valjean suspects he finally has met his doom. Javert pulls out his gun and looks at Valjean with a face furrowed with frustration. "You're a difficult problem," he callously tells Valjean, and he orders him to the concrete precipice overhanging the river.

Uneasy about Javert's plans, Valjean asks, "Why aren't you taking me in?"

Irritated by Valjean's inquisitiveness, Javert crossly commands, "You are my prisoner. Do what I tell you." Shaking his head incredulously, he continues, "You don't understand the importance of the law. I've given you an order. Obey it."

The loaded gun now aimed at his chest, Valjean does as he is ordered. He turns toward the river. Although he can't see Javert, he feels the barrel of his gun now coolly resting on his cheek; one click of the trigger, and Javert will finally defeat his enemy.

But Javert is still riddled as to why Valjean freed him from the rebels. He asks, "Why didn't you kill me?"

Blankly, Valjean responds, "I don't have the right to kill you."

"But you hate me," Javert reasons.

"I don't hate you," Valjean impassively continues. "I don't feel anything."

Miffed by Valjean's response, Javert threatens, "You don't want to go back to the quarries, do you?"

Valjean stands in silence, recalling his previous stint in a hard-labor prison. He shakes his head. Surely a swift death would be better.

"Then for once we agree," Javert concludes. "I'm going to spare you from a life in prison, Jean Valjean. It's a pity the rules don't allow me to be merciful."

The barrel of the gun now corkscrewing beneath his chin, Valjean waits for his death.

In a tone of tired resignation, Javert says, "I've tried to live my life without breaking a single rule." Then, without warning, Javert drops his gun and undoes Valjean's handcuffs. Javert shoves Valjean to the ground in frustration. He sneers, "You're free."

Unable to live a life where the law is weakened by mercy, Javert handcuffs himself and plunges backwards into the river. Valjean stands in disbelief as he watches his foe descend into the deep waters.

Valjean is finally free.

Elapsed time: Measured from the beginning of the opening credit, this scene begins at 02:05:40 and lasts approximately three and one-half minutes.

Content: Rated PG-13 for some violence and language

Citation: *Les Misérables* (Columbia Pictures, 1998), written by Rafael Yglesias (based on the novel *Les Misérables* by Victor Hugo), directed by Bille August

submitted by Melissa Parks, Des Plaines, Illinois

67. NEW LIFE

Air Force One

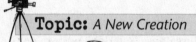

Topic: *A New Creation*

Texts: *2 Corinthians 5:17; Galatians 2:20; Ephesians 4:21–24*

Keywords: *Born Again; Christian; Christian Life; Conversion; Identity in Christ; Indwelling of Christ; New Life; New Man; Regeneration*

In the movie *Air Force One,* the president of the United States (played by Harrison Ford) is taken hostage as terrorists hijack his official aircraft, Air Force One. Drawing on his former military experience, the president eventually kills or disables all the terrorists but one.

The crisis, however, is far from over. There is no one left who can safely land the plane. The vice president and the joint chiefs of staff are working together in a tension-filled White House war room to develop a strategy for what appears to be a hopeless situation. As time runs out, the only viable solution is a daring rescue in which the air force will attempt to attach a zip line—a metal cable with a pulley attachment—from Air Force One to a military transport plane. Someone could then hook himself to the pulley and ride the zip line from one plane to the other. For such a rescue to succeed, precision is essential.

All of the passengers make it safely to the transport plane, leaving the president and one terrorist aboard Air Force One. Just before the president hooks himself to the life-saving zip line, the terrorist comes out of hiding and a struggle ensues. Shortly thereafter, Air Force One dives into the ocean.

The officials on the ground wait anxiously through long periods of radio silence. Unable to see what is transpiring, they all gather anxiously around the radio for a report from the military flight crew. All they know from their radar screen is that Air Force One is down. A sense of defeat permeates the room as they assume that the president has gone down with the plane.

Finally, the flight crew radios the anxious officials gathered in the White House war room, saying, "Liberty 2–4 is changing call signs. Liberty 2–4 is now Air Force One!" The president had been pulled safely aboard the cargo plane just before his jet plunged into the ocean.

The identity of the simple transport plane was dramatically changed—from Liberty 2–4 to Air Force One—when the president came on board. So, too, we experience a profound change of identity when Jesus Christ comes into our life.

Elapsed time: This scene begins at 01:56:24 and goes to 01:57:14.

Content: Rated R for heavy violence, suspenseful scenes, and some profanity

Citation: *Air Force One* (Columbia Pictures, 1997), written by Andrew W. Marlowe, directed by Wolfgang Petersen

cited in a sermon by James Shaddix II, New Orleans, Louisiana; submitted by David Slagle, Lawrenceville, Georgia

68. PARENTING

Jack Frost

Topic: *How Parents Leave Their Mark on the World*

Texts: *Deuteronomy 6:4–7; Psalm 127:3–5;*
2 Timothy 1:5

Keywords: *Achievement; Career; Children; Fatherhood;*
Fathers; Meaning of Life; Parenting; Priorities; Raising
Children; Success; Time; Work

Set in snowy central Colorado, *Jack Frost* is an adaptation of the Christmas song "Frosty the Snowman." Michael Keaton plays a dad named Jack Frost, who struggles to balance his career with parenthood. He is on the verge of fulfilling his lifelong dream as a musician—signing with a record company—but he spends more time in the studio than with his eleven-year-old son, Charlie (played by Joseph Cross).

After missing one of Charlie's hockey games, Jack tries to make things right. He promises a Christmas vacation in a cabin up north without any interruptions. The next day, however, Jack gets "the" phone call from a record company interested in signing his band. Jack and his wife, Gabby (played by Kelly Preston), formulate a plan for Jack to drive to Aspen, perform with his band on Christmas Day, and then drive back to the cabin to be with his family.

Charlie is crushed, but Jack follows his ambition. On the road to Aspen, he thinks about what he's doing to his son, changes his mind, and heads back. Tragically, a blinding snowstorm and faulty windshield wipers cause an accident that kills Jack.

A year later, Charlie and Gabby are still coping with Jack's death. Charlie decides to build a snowman—one of the few things he and his dad enjoyed doing together. Suddenly, the balls of snow are inhabited by Jack's spirit, and he's transformed into a snowman. Once Charlie works through his initial shock, he helps his dad get to the family cabin before he melts. Following an eventful day, Charlie falls asleep, and Jack tucks his son in for the night.

He thinks back to his life as a human, strokes his son's hair, and says, "I was so busy trying to make my mark on the world that . . ." and he trails off, pausing to reflect. Then, just before he bends down to kiss his son on the forehead, he says, "You are my mark on the world."

Elapsed time: Measured from the beginning of the opening credit, this scene begins at 01:28:12 and ends at 01:28:38.

Content: Rated PG for mild violence, language, and bathroom sexuality

Citation: *Jack Frost* (Warner Brothers, 1998), written by Mark Steven Johnson, Steven Bloom, Jonathan Roberts, and Jeff Cesario, directed by Troy Miller

submitted by Clark Cothern, Tecumseh, Michigan

Bonhoeffer: Agent of Grace

Topic: Bonhoeffer's Prayer Brings Prisoner Peace

Texts: Psalm 22; Philippians 4:6–7

Keywords: Attitudes and Emotions; Belief; Conversion; Courage; Death; Despair; Faith; Fear; Hope; Loneliness; Love; Ministry; Peace; Prayer; Unbelief

The made for TV film, *Bonhoeffer: Agent of Grace,* depicts the life and death of Dietrich Bonhoeffer, a leader in the Confessing Church of Germany during the 1940s. Bonhoeffer opposed Adolf Hitler's government and was arrested and sentenced to death by the Nazi regime.

As Bonhoeffer (played by Ulrich Tukur) lies in his darkened prison cell, he hears through the concrete wall the weeping of a prisoner in the adjacent cell. Speaking through the wall, Bonhoeffer identifies himself as a pastor, assures the man that he is not alone, and asks if he would like to pray. The muffled reply comes back: "I don't believe in God."

When a German guard looks in and learns that Bonhoeffer is trying to pray with his neighbor, he responds, "Kitchner? It won't do any good. He's going to be shot any day now."

Undaunted, Bonhoeffer leans against the stark cell wall and calls out to the prisoner, "If you can hear me, put your hands on the wall as if we were touching. Mine are here too." No hands appear.

As the guard looks on through a peephole, Bonhoeffer prays, "Lord, it's dark in me; in you is day. I am alone, but you will stay. I am afraid; you never cease. I am at war; in you is peace." Slowly we see a pair of hands reach up and touch the wall opposite of where Bonhoeffer's hands are.

As dawn breaks, a single rifle shot shatters the morning calm. The same German guard, now more somber and less cynical, appears at Bonhoeffer's cell. "I thought you might like to know. The boy from the next cell—he was very calm. It surprised everyone. He was executed this morning."

Elapsed time: The scene lasts a little under three and one-half minutes, running from 00:44:29 to 00:47:50.

Content: Not rated, but it does contain mature themes

Citation: *Bonhoeffer: Agent of Grace* (Gateway Films, 1999), written by Gareth Jones and Eric Till, directed by Eric Till

submitted by Stephen Nordbye, Charlton, Massachusetts

70. PEACE

The Shawshank Redemption

Topic: *Shielded by Peace*

Texts: *Psalm 18; John 14:27; Romans 8:31; Philippians 4:7*

Keywords: *Abundant Life; Adversity; Anxiety; Attitude; Cheerfulness; Christian Life; Comforter; Contentment; Discouragement; Freedom; Overcoming; Peace; Prisons; Protection; Renewal; Renewing the Mind; Security in God; Thoughts*

In the feature film *The Shawshank Redemption*, Ellis "Red" Redding (played by Morgan Freeman) tells the story of Andy Dufresne (played by Tim Robbins)—a successful young banker who is wrongly convicted of murdering his wife in 1947 and sentenced to two consecutive life prison terms at Shawshank Prison. Andy endures confinement year after year while maintaining his hope for freedom.

Red is a hardened but somewhat repentant convict resigned to spending the rest of his natural life behind the gray prison walls. When Red first sees Andy arrive at Shawshank, he takes an immediate disliking to the tall, slender banker. According to Red, Andy looked weak—"like a stiff breeze would blow him over." In fact, Red gambled that Andy would be the first of the new prisoners to break down. Surprisingly, Andy survives his first tormented night at Shawshank with his sanity intact, and not long afterwards, he meets Red in the prison yard for the first time.

As Andy strolls away from his conversation with Red, he stoops to collect a pebble from the dusty prison grounds; the bright sunlight seems to transform his drab prison uniform into casual wear. Red reflects in a voice-over: *I can see why some of the boys took him for snobby. He had a quiet way about him—a walk and a talk that just wasn't normal around here. He strolled like a man in the park, without a care or a worry in the world. Like he had on an invisible coat that would shield him from this place.*

There is a way we can live like Andy Dufresne—an innocent man placed in difficult circumstances, shielded by a mysterious peace. *God* can be our peace, our invisible coat shielding us from trouble.

Elapsed time: Measured from the beginning of the opening credit, the first scene begins at 00:11:45 and ends at 00:12:00; the second scene begins at 00:28:16 and ends at 00:28:46.

Content: Rated R for profanity and violence

Citation: *The Shawshank Redemption* (Castle Rock, 1994), written by Frank Darabont (based on the novella *Rita Hayworth and Shawshank Redemption* by Stephen King), directed by Frank Darabont

submitted by Rich Tatum, Romeoville, Illinois

71. PERCEPTION AND REALITY

The Matrix

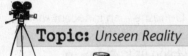

Topic: *Unseen Reality*

Texts: *Luke 24:13–35; Romans 6:16–23; Ephesians 6:12; 1 Peter 1:13–21*

Keywords: *Bondage; Discernment; Knowledge and Knowing; Perception and Reality; Seen and Unseen; Slavery; Spiritual Warfare; Truth; World*

In the science-fiction movie *The Matrix,* the real world has been taken over by computers that keep humans in bondage by creating a false reality in their minds. The computers electronically feed a virtual reality into their brains. The humans think they are free, but they are actually entombed in pods where their bodies are used as an energy source.

A few of the humans have escaped their pods and are battling the machines. But unlike the computer-induced dreamland (called the Matrix), the real world is full of sweat, stress, and combat with the computers at every turn.

In one scene, the leader of escaped humans—Morpheus (played by Laurence Fishburne)—has contacted a person whose mind is still controlled by the Matrix. The man's name is Neo (played by Keanu Reeves).

"Let me tell you why you're here," says Morpheus. "You're here because you know something. What you know you can't explain—but you feel it. You've felt it your entire life. That there's something wrong with the world. You don't know what it is, but it's there, like a splinter in your mind, driving you mad. It is this feeling that has brought you to me. Do you know what I'm talking about?"

"The Matrix?" Neo asks.

"Do you want to know what it is?" asks Morpheus. Neo nods. "The Matrix is everywhere. It is all around us. Even now in this very room. You can see it when you look out your window or when you turn on your television. You can feel it when you go to work, when you go to church, when you pay your taxes. It is the world that has been pulled over your eyes to blind you from the truth."

"What truth?" asks Neo.

"That you are a slave, Neo. Like everyone else, you were born into bondage. Born into a prison that you cannot smell or taste or touch—a prison for your mind. Unfortunately, no one can be told what the Matrix is. You have to see it for yourself." Morpheus takes out two pills—one blue, one red. "This is your last chance. After this there is no turning back. You take the blue pill—the story ends, and you wake up in your bed and believe whatever you want to believe. You take the red pill—you stay in Wonderland and I show you how deep the rabbit hole goes. Remember, all I'm offering is the truth, nothing more."

Neo chooses the red pill, and the Matrix starts to break down. He sees the world for how it really is. He realizes that the truth is a war between good and evil and that the allures of this world are nothing but an illusion.

Elapsed time: This scene begins at 00:26:36 and lasts approximately four minutes.

Content: Rated R for excessive violence and some language

Citation: *The Matrix* (Warner Brothers, 1999), written and directed by Andy and Larry Wachowski

submitted by Bill White, Paramount, California

72. PLANNING

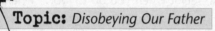

Fiddler on the Roof

Topic: *Disobeying Our Father*

Texts: *1 Samuel 12:15; 1 Samuel 13:13–14; 1 Samuel 15:10–29; Isaiah 30:1; 1 John 5:14–15*

Keywords: *Blessings; Desire; Disobedience; Human Nature; Human Will; Obedience; Planning; Plans; Prayer; Rebellion; Self-Will*

The movie *Fiddler on the Roof* tells of a poor Jewish father's struggle to cling to tradition in an ever-changing world. The main character, Tevye (played by Topol), is a father of five girls who scrapes out a meager living delivering milk. Most troubling for Tevye are the choices his daughters make concerning marriage. Tradition dictated that marriages would be arranged. But Tevye's oldest daughter desires to choose her own husband. After much discussion, Tevye reluctantly agrees.

Tevye's second daughter, Hodel (played by Michelle Marsh), decides that she, too, will choose her own husband, a young revolutionary named Perchik (played by Michael Glaser). Perchik has no use for tradition and, true to his character, asks Hodel to marry him without consulting Tevye. Hodel and Perchik are radiant with glee; the sun is the only thing brighter than the newly engaged couple as they stroll hand in hand down an old dirt road. Their countenances change quickly, however, as they unexpectedly run into Tevye, who looks askance at the two lovers holding hands as he sets down his cart.

Perchik, nervous, begins the awkward conversation. "I have some bad news," Perchik tells Tevye. "I must leave here."

"When?" asks Tevye, looking truly dismayed.

Smiling, Perchik tells Tevye, "You'll have to congratulate me!"

Tevye broadly smiles and extends his hand to shake Perchik's hand before he hears the news. "What for?" Tevye asks, shaking Perchik's hand vigorously.

Perchik drops the bomb: "We are engaged!"

Immediately Tevye pulls his hand back, and his smile quickly turns to a glower. "Oh, no, you're not," says Tevye. He says to his daughter, "I know you like him and he likes you, but you're going away, Perchik, and, [Hodel], you're staying here. So have a nice trip, Perchik, and I hope you'll be very happy, and my answer is no!"

A tearful Hodel pleads with her father, but Tevye stands firm in his decision. All the bickering quickly ceases, however, when Perchik declares, "But, Tevye, we are not asking for your permission, only your blessing." Tevye seems barely aware of his surroundings as he attempts to absorb what Perchik has just said.

Astonished, Tevye looks at the couple and asks, "You're not asking for my permission?"

Hodel responds, "But we would like your blessing, Papa."

"I can't believe my ears," says Tevye. "My blessing? For what? For going over my head? Impossible! At least with Tzeitel and Motel they asked me. They begged me. But now, if I like it or not, you marry him?"

In a similar way, we may deal with God as Perchik dealt with Tevye. We ask for our Father's blessing rather than for his permission.

Elapsed time: Measured from the beginning of the opening credit, this scene begins at 02:00:06 and ends at 02:02:44.

Content: Rated G

Citation: *Fiddler on the Roof* (United Artists, 1971), written by Joseph Stein (based on the short story "Tevye and His Daughters" by Sholom Aleichem), directed by Norman Jewison

submitted by David Slagle, Lawrenceville, Georgia

73. PLEASING GOD

Chariots of Fire

Topic: *Using Our Abilities to Honor God*

Texts: *John 4:34; John 8:29; Romans 12:4–8;
1 Corinthians 12; Ephesians 4:11–16;
Ephesians 5:10; Colossians 3:23–25;
1 Timothy 4:14–15; 1 Peter 4:10–11*

Keywords: *Calling; Competition; Faithfulness; Joy;
Ministry; Missions; Pleasing God; Service; Spiritual Gifts;
Sports*

Chariots of Fire is the true story of two British runners competing in the 1924 Olympics. Eric Liddell (played by Ian Charleson) is a devout Christian and one of the finest runners in the world. Eric's sister, Jennie (played by Cheryl Campbell), wants him to leave competitive running to join the family on the mission field in China. Jennie thinks Eric is putting running ahead of serving God, and she questions his commitment.

In one scene, Eric attempts to help his sister see his point of view.

Eric announces with a smile, "I've decided I'm going back to China. The missionary service has accepted . . ."

Jennie interrupts him. "Oh, Eric, I'm so pleased."

Eric continues, "But I've got a lot of running to do first. Jennie, you've got to understand. I believe that God made me for a purpose—for China. He also made me fast, and when I run, I feel his pleasure. To give it up would be to hold him in contempt. You were right. It's not just fun. To win is to honor him."

Elapsed time: Measured from the beginning of the opening credit, this scene begins at 00:58:24 and lasts about one and one-half minutes.

Content: Rated PG

Citation: *Chariots of Fire* (Warner Brothers, 1981), written by Colin Welland, directed by Hugh Hudson

submitted by Greg Asimakoupoulos, Naperville, Illinois, and Doug Scott, Elgin, Illinois

74. PRAYER

Shadowlands

Topic: *Prayer Changes Us*

Texts: *Psalm 5:1–3; Matthew 6:7–8; John 14:13–14; Colossians 4:2; 1 Timothy 2:1–4; James 1:6–8; 1 John 5:14–15*

Keywords: *God's Will; Human Will; Prayer; Prayer in God's Will; Submission; Trust*

Shadowlands portrays the joy and pain of the relationship between C. S. Lewis (played by Anthony Hopkins) and American writer Joy Gresham (played by Debra Winger). A growing friendship led to a marriage of convenience. The Oxford professor wed the single mother in a secret civil ceremony so that Joy could gain English citizenship. Eventually it was discovered that Joy had terminal cancer, and Lewis realized that he really did love her.

Joy's cancer went into temporary remission, and for a season she and Lewis experienced the depth of committed Christian love. During this time, an Anglican priest talked with Lewis about prayer. In their conversation, we hear a mature description of how prayer works.

The priest said, "I know how hard you've been praying. And now God is answering your prayer."

Lewis responded, "That's not why I pray, Harry. I pray because I can't help myself. I pray because I'm helpless. I pray because the need flows out of me all the time—waking and sleeping. It doesn't change God; it changes me."

Elapsed time: Measured from the beginning of the opening credit, this scene begins at 01:29:35 and goes to 01:30:15.

Content: Rated PG

Citation: *Shadowlands* (Savoy Pictures, 1993), written by William Nicholson, directed by Richard Attenborough

submitted by Greg Asimakoupoulos, Naperville, Illinois, and Doug Scott, Elgin, Illinois

75. PROVIDENCE

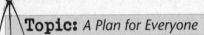

Simon Birch

Topic: *A Plan for Everyone*

Texts: *Exodus 4:11; Isaiah 45:7–10; Jeremiah 29:11; Lamentations 3:38; John 9:3; Romans 8:28; Philippians 1:6; Philippians 2:12–13; Hebrews 10:36; 1 Peter 4:10*

Keywords: *Attitude; Belief; Calling; Childlike Faith; Circumstances and Faith; Confidence; Destiny; Disabilities; Doubt; Faith; God's Will; Providence; Purpose; Skepticism; Trust; Weakness*

Simon Birch (loosely based on John Irving's *A Prayer for Owen Meany*) tells the story of a twelve-year-old boy named Simon Birch (played by Ian Michael Smith) who, despite his physical disabilities, believes that God has a plan for his life. Simon was born tiny and with an abnormally small heart. He was expected to die within the first twenty-four hours of his life. He surprises everyone, though, when he lives to be an adolescent.

A disappointment to his parents and the target of many childhood pranks because of his miniature size and odd-sounding voice, Simon has every reason to question his self-worth and purpose for living. But he embraces his condition and believes that God will use him in a unique, possibly even heroic, way.

Joe (played by Joseph Mazzello), Simon's best friend, doesn't believe in God, and he is not the only one who doubts that God has a plan for Simon. Simon's schoolmates mock him relentlessly, believing his assertions to be one more indication of his strangeness. On one occasion his Sunday school teacher hurriedly tries to hush him so he won't "frighten" the other children with his musings.

The small town's forlorn minister (played by David Strathairn) also doubts that God could have a plan for small Simon Birch. In a poignant conversation between Simon and the minister, Simon asks, "Does God have a plan for us?"

The minister hesitantly replies, "I like to think he does."

Simon enthusiastically says, "Me too. I think God made me the way I am for a reason."

The minister coolly states, "I'm glad that, um, that your faith, uh, helps you deal with your, um, you know, your condition."

"That's not what I mean," Simon states. "I think I'm God's instrument. He's going to use me to carry out his plan."

Dumbfounded by Simon's confidence, the pastor says, "It's wonderful to have faith, son, but let's not overdo it." With that he waves for Simon to leave, shakes his head in disbelief, and whispers with an air of cynicism, "God's instrument."

A short time later Simon is riding with his classmates in a school bus traveling down an icy road. Suddenly the bus driver veers to avoid a deer, loses control, and the bus plunges into an icy lake. Everyone in the front of the upright bus quickly evacuates out the door, but Simon and a handful of other students in the back of the bus are trapped as the bus begins to sink.

Simon takes charge. He opens a window and commands his classmates to climb out. Last of all, Simon escapes through the window.

In the hospital following the accident, Joe assures Simon that all the kids are all right. Simon asks, "Did you see how the children listened to me because of the way I looked?"

Joe, with tears in his eyes, replies, "Yeah."

With satisfaction, Simon says, "That window was just my size."

"Extra small," Joe utters with a smile.

A few seconds later, Simon dies, knowing that God used him. But what Simon doesn't know before he dies is that because of his unwavering faith, his friend Joe now believes in God.

Some twenty years later, standing at Simon's gravestone, Joe says, "I am doomed to remember a boy with a wrecked voice, not because of his voice or because he was the smallest person I ever met . . . but because he is the reason I believe in God. What faith I have, I owe to Simon Birch—it is Simon who made me a believer."

Elapsed time: Measured from when the studio logo appears, the scene between Simon and his minister begins at 01:07:23 and lasts fifty-six seconds; the final scene between Simon and Joe begins at 01:43:50 and lasts approximately three minutes.

Content: Rated PG for language

Citation: *Simon Birch* (Hollywood Pictures, 1998), written and directed by Mark Steven Johnson (loosely based on the novel *A Prayer for Owen Meany* by John Irving)

submitted by Melissa Parks, Des Plaines, Illinois

76. PURPOSE

Antz

Topic: *Search for Significance*

Texts: *Psalm 8; Psalm 139:13–16; Ecclesiastes 1:1–11; Matthew 6:26–30; Matthew 10:31; Matthew 12:12; Romans 8:14–39; 1 Corinthians 12:14–18; Ephesians 1:11; Ephesians 2:10; Philippians 1:6; Philippians 2:13*

Keywords: *Attitude; Calling; Destiny; Individualism; Insignificance; Meaning of Life; Purpose; Self-Worth; Servanthood; Significance; Work*

In an early scene from the animated movie *Antz*, the camera pans down from a faraway view of a big city to blades of grass to below the grass and into a room. The main character, an ant named Z (starring the voice of Woody Allen), lies on a leaf couch and tells his therapist, "All my life I've lived and worked in the big city. . . . I always tell myself there has got to be something better out there. Maybe I, maybe I think too much. I think everything must go back to the fact that I had a very anxious childhood. My mother never had time for me. When you're the middle child in a family of five million, you don't get any attention. I mean, how is it possible? I've always had these abandonment issues, which plagued me. My father was basically a drone, like I've said. The guy flew away when I was just a larva.

"And my job, don't get me started on it because it really annoys me. I was not cut out to be a worker. I, I feel physically inadequate. My whole life I've never been able to lift more than ten times my own body weight. And, and, when you get down to it, handling dirt is not my idea of a rewarding career. . . . I mean, what is it—I'm supposed to do everything for the colony? What about my needs? What about me? I mean I've got to believe there's some place out there that's better than this. Otherwise I'll just curl up into a larva position and weep. The whole system makes me feel . . . insignificant."

The therapist responds, "Excellent! You've made a real breakthrough!"

Z says, "I have?"

"Yes, Z. You are insignificant!" replies the therapist.

The scene shifts, and millions of worker ants are shown all doing the same work. An elaborate network of tunnels is used by endless lines of ants carrying pieces of dirt. In one area, newborn ants are assigned their lot in life. In assembly-line style, one newborn ant is labeled "worker" and given a pickax. The next one is labeled "soldier" and given a military helmet.

As Z goes to his workstation, he says to himself, "OK, I've just got to keep a positive attitude. A good attitude—even though I'm utterly insignificant. I'm insignificant, but with attitude."

Elapsed time: This scene begins the movie and lasts approximately five minutes.

Content: Rated PG for language and menacing action

Citation: *Antz* (DreamWorks, 1998), written by Todd Alcott, Chris Weitz, and Paul Weitz, directed by Eric Darnell and Tim Johnson

submitted by Jerry De Luca,
Montreal West, Quebec, Canada

77. RACISM

Cry, the Beloved Country

Topic: *Sacrifice to Battle Prejudice*

Texts: *Exodus 22:21; Luke 10:25–37; Luke 14:12–14; John 13:1–17; John 13:34–35; Acts 10:28; Romans 15:7; 1 Corinthians 13:1–7; Colossians 3:11; 1 John 2:9–11; 1 John 4:19–21; Revelation 7:9*

Keywords: Bigotry; Brotherhood; Brotherly Love; Caring; Character; Commitment; Community; Compassion; Convictions; Courage; Death; Family; Fathers; Giving; Grief; Human Help; Injustice; Legacy; Loss; Ministry; Prejudice; Racism; Sacrifice; Service; Sorrow

Cry, the Beloved Country, set in 1946 South Africa, tells the story of a black minister (played by James Earl Jones) who must deal with his son's unintentional murder of a white man during a home burglary. The murdered white man is the son of James Jarvis (played by Richard Harris), a wealthy and racist South African farmer.

In this scene, James Jarvis visits an all-black athletic club that was founded, financed, and operated by his recently murdered son. The large sign in front of the old building reads CLAREMONT AFRICAN BOYS CLUB. Jarvis enters a large room where several young men are boxing, punching a bag, or working out. Pictures of boxers decorate the deteriorating walls. All the athletes stop and stare at the white man in his immaculate business suit. Jarvis notices a nameplate on the wall with his son's name and the title PRESIDENT below his photograph. He stares at the picture of his son posing with several members of the club. A middle-aged black man dressed in a suit walks over to him.

"Can I help you, sir? My name is Robert Dentela. I'm a teacher."

Jarvis replies, "I'm Arthur's father."

Robert turns to the young men. "It's a friend. Carry on."

Then Robert addresses Jarvis, who is pensively staring at the photo with the back of his hand resting on his forehead: "I'm sorry for your loss, sir. I'm afraid . . . I've no office, but I . . . We were never able to thank him properly. He bought us . . . (motioning with his hand) he bought us all this. They were small things, sir. What your son truly gave to us was himself—his time, his heart, his belief in a better future."

Jarvis sits on the bench below the photograph and says, "Yes, I've read some of the things he said he believed in."

Sitting beside Jarvis, Robert says, "Sir, to my knowledge your son never said he believed in something unless he believed it."

Jarvis stares straight ahead. "I would like nothing better than to understand my boy."

"He's the only man I ever met, black or white," replies Robert, "who saw me for what I am. What I really am."

Standing up with an impatient expression on his face, Jarvis says, "Yes. He was on your side. Which makes what happened . . ."

Robert interrupted. "He was on no one's side, sir. Perhaps yours and mine. You must be proud of him. He's a tribute to you."

Elapsed time: Measured from the studio logo, the scene begins at 00:55:52 and goes to 00:59:55.

Content: Rated PG-13 for emotional intensity and language

Citation: *Cry, the Beloved Country* (Miramax Films, 1995), written by Ronald Harwood (based on the novel by Alan Paton), directed by Darrell James Roodt

submitted by Jerry De Luca,
Montreal West, Quebec, Canada

78. RECONCILIATION

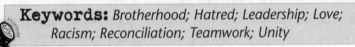

Remember the Titans

Topic: *Hatred Turns into Love*

Texts: *Romans 15:7; 1 John 2:9–11; 1 John 4:19–21*

Keywords: *Brotherhood; Hatred; Leadership; Love; Racism; Reconciliation; Teamwork; Unity*

Remember the Titans is based on the true story of a Virginia high school football team's climb to the top. The movie also tells of a team's ability, and ultimately an entire town's ability, to deal with racial integration in 1971. Because of government-mandated redistricting, black students and white students, for the first time in their lives, had to attend the same high school.

Early in the movie Gary (played by Ryan Hurst), a white athlete, and Julius (played by Wood Harris), a black athlete, display overt racial hostility toward one another. Gary is an all-American football player and Julius is a star defensive player. At a two-week long summer camp, Gary and Julius are assigned a room together. When Julius puts a poster on the wall that depicts several black athletes winning Olympic medals, Gary says, "I'm not looking at that for two weeks."

Julius responds, "Well, you better get some X-ray vision, Superman."

When Gary attempts to rip the poster off the wall, a brawl ensues between the black and white players. Just when it seems that the two groups will never overcome their animosity toward one another, Gary and Julius have a heart-to-heart conversation. Julius confronts Gary regarding Gary's silence when white team members deliberately miss blocks for black players. During the next practice, Gary confronts a white player for this behavior. His act of leadership is a catalyst for change for the rest of the team.

Initially, their motivation to reconcile appears to be based on their mutual desire to win football games. Later, however, they are motivated by something stronger. After the Titans win the regional championship, Gary is involved in a serious car accident that leaves him paralyzed from the waist down. The entire football team is at the hospital, but Gary requests to see only Julius. Mustering all the emotional strength he has, Julius walks into the room. A nurse immediately responds, "Only kin are allowed in here."

Gary reassures her, "It's all right, Alice." Jokingly, he continues, "Can't you see the family resemblance? He's my brother."

There is laughter—but there is truth to the comment. As Julius stands at Gary's bedside, Gary says, "When I first met you, I was scared of you, Julius. I only saw what I was afraid of." Through tears he confesses, "But then I saw I was only hating my brother."

Elapsed time: Measured from the beginning of the opening credit, this scene begins at 01:27:20 and lasts two minutes.

Content: Rated PG for thematic elements and mild profanity

Citation: *Remember the Titans* (Disney, 2000), written by Gregory Allen Howard, directed by Boaz Yakin

submitted by David Slagle, Lawrenceville, Georgia

79. RECONCILIATION

The Straight Story

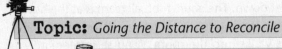

Topic: *Going the Distance to Reconcile*

Texts: *John 3:16; Romans 5:8; 2 Corinthians 5:18; 1 Timothy 1:15*

Keywords: *Christmas; Christ's Forgiveness; Christ's Love; Family; Forgiveness; Peace; Reconciliation; Relationships*

The Straight Story (based on a true story) chronicles a seventy-three-year-old man's pilgrimage to mend a broken relationship with his brother, Lyle, whom he hasn't seen or spoken to in over ten years. When Alvin Straight (played by Richard Farnsworth) learns that Lyle (played by Harry Dean Stanton) has had a stroke, he determines to visit him and make things right.

Alvin hitches a makeshift trailer to his 1966 John Deere riding lawn mower and sets out on a five-hundred-mile trip. He camps out in fields and backyards made available by hospitable people he meets along the way. Slowly but surely, Alvin perseveres and reaches his brother.

He steers his riding mower down a dirt road and finds a run-down wooden shack. Alvin climbs off the mower, shuffles slowly toward the house, and calls out, "Lyle! Lyle!" There is no response. The look on Alvin's furrowed face gives evidence to his fear. Perhaps he's too late—maybe Lyle has died in the six weeks since he began his journey.

After a lengthy pause, a voice from inside the shack calls, "Alvin? Alvin?" Lyle appears at the front door holding on to a walker. He invites Alvin to join him on the porch, where they silently sit. Alvin nervously looks at his brother, while Lyle studies the riding mower and makeshift trailer. Obviously overcome with emotion and grati-tude, his eyes puddle as he asks, "You came all this way on that—just to see me?"

Alvin's face twitches, betraying his emotion. His eyes, too, are tearful. He smiles and simply says, "Yep!"

Lyle's face speaks for his heart. He is humbled by his brother's grace.

Elapsed time: Measured from the beginning of the opening credit, this scene begins at 01:44:00 and lasts approximately three and one-half minutes.

Content: Rated G

Citation: *The Straight Story* (Disney, 1999), written by John Roach and Mary Sweeney (based on the story of the real-life Alvin Straight), directed by David Lynch

submitted by Greg Asimakoupoulos, Naperville, Illinois

80. RECONCILIATION

The Straight Story

Topic: *Yearning for Reconciliation*

Texts: *Genesis 4:1–12; Matthew 5:21–24; Matthew 6:14–15; Matthew 7:1–5; Mark 9:50; Luke 15; Luke 19:10; John 20:23; Romans 14:19; Ephesians 4:32; Colossians 3:13*

Keywords: *Bitterness; Brotherly Love; Conflict; Courage; Desire; Determination; Family; Forgiveness; Peacemakers; Perseverance; Reconciliation; Relationships; Second Chances; Sin*

The movie *The Straight Story* is based on a true story and chronicles the pilgrimage of a seventy-three-year-old man to mend a broken relationship with his brother, whom he hasn't seen or spoken to in over ten years. Alvin Straight (played by Richard Farnsworth) lives in Laurens, Iowa.

Alvin has lost his driver's license because of impaired vision. When a call comes reporting that Lyle (played by Harry Dean Stanton), Alvin's estranged brother, has had a stroke, Alvin determines to find a way to visit his brother and make things right. His only solution is to hitch a makeshift trailer to his 1966 John Deere riding lawn mower and set out on a five-hundred-mile trip that will take him in excess of six weeks. Camping out in fields and backyards made available by hospitable people, Alvin Straight slowly but surely makes his way toward his destination. After crossing the Mississippi River and entering Wisconsin, Alvin camps out in a church cemetery, kindling a campfire between tombstones. The pastor of the adjoining church (played by John Lordan) sees Alvin from his office, has pity on the "homeless" man, and brings him a plate of hot meat loaf and mashed potatoes. A conversation ensues.

"I can't help but notice your rather unlikely mode of transportation," the pastor says eyeing the riding mower. Alvin makes mention of his brother who lives in the area. The pastor recalls having met a man by that name while making calls in the hospital but admits that he didn't recall the man making mention of having a brother.

"Neither one of us has had a brother for quite some time," Alvin explained. "Lyle and I grew up as close as brothers could be. We were raised in Moorhead, Minnesota. We worked hard. . . . Me and Lyle would make games out of our chores. . . . He and I used to sleep out in the yard most every summer night. We talked to each other till we went to sleep. It made our trials seem smaller. We pretty much talked each other through growing up."

The pastor asked, "Whatever happened between you two?"

Alvin's eyes tear up as he explains, "The story's as old as Cain and Abel. Anger. Vanity. Mix that together with liquor, and you've got two brothers who haven't spoken in ten years."

Alvin's manner and voice indicate the depth to which he is grieving the barrier that exists between him and Lyle. He adds, "Whatever it was that made me and Lyle so mad, it doesn't matter anymore. I want to make peace and sit with him and look up at the stars like we used to do."

Like Alvin, many of us have someone with whom we deeply long to be reconciled.

Elapsed time: Measured from the beginning of the opening credit, the scene begins at 01:32:00 and lasts about four and one-half minutes.

Content: Rated G

Citation: *The Straight Story* (Disney, 1999), written by John Roach and Mary Sweeney (based on the story of the real-life Alvin Straight), directed by David Lynch

submitted by Greg Asimakoupoulos, Naperville, Illinois

81. REDEMPTION

Les Misérables

Topic: *Redeemed by Love*

Texts: *Luke 6:27–36; John 8:1–11; Acts 20:28; 1 Corinthians 6:20; 1 Corinthians 7:23; Colossians 1:12–14; 1 Timothy 2:6; Hebrews 9:15; 2 Peter 2:1; Revelation 5:9; Revelation 14:4*

Keywords: *Atonement; Compassion; Conversion; Forgiveness; Grace; Mercy; New Life; New Man; Redeemer; Redemption; Repentance; Sacrifice; Salvation*

The movie *Les Misérables,* based on the famous novel by Victor Hugo, opens with a vagabond curled up on a stone bench on a desolate French street corner. His bedraggled appearance makes him seem dangerous and causes the townspeople, from whom he sought food and shelter, to snub him. Finally he slumps over in dejection—until a passerby points to a place where he can find refuge.

He goes to the door and knocks. The homeowner—the town's bishop—is startled by the late-night visitation but attentively listens to his story. The vagabond's name is Jean Valjean (played by Liam Neeson), and he reveals that he is a recently released convict and marked by the authorities as dangerous. Even so, the bishop (played by Peter Vaughan) welcomes him into his home and serves him dinner.

Later, in the middle of the night, despite the bishop's kindness, Valjean double-crosses him. Valjean remembers the sparkling silver spoon he used to eat his soup at dinner and sneaks into the dining room to steal the bishop's valuable silverware. The clanking of metal arouses the bishop, who rises to inspect the clattering below. When they meet face-to-face, Valjean strikes the bishop, leaving him unconscious, and escapes with a heavy knapsack of silver.

The following morning the bishop's wife laments the loss of her silver, but the bishop seems unperturbed, telling his wife, "So we'll use wooden spoons. I don't want to hear anything more about it." Moments later, authorities appear at the bishop's manor with the stolen silver and a handcuffed Valjean.

Looking deeply into the thief's eyes, the bishop says, "I'm very angry with you, Jean Valjean." Turning toward the authorities, he asks, "Didn't he tell you he was our guest?"

"Oh, yes," replies the chief authority, "after we searched his knapsack and found all this silver. He claimed that you gave it to him."

Stooping in shame, Valjean expects the bishop to indict him. A new prison sentence awaits him. But the bishop says, "Yes. Of course I gave him the silverware." Then, looking intently at Valjean he asks, "But why didn't you take the candlesticks? That was very foolish. They're worth at least two thousand francs. Why did you leave them? Did you forget to take them?"

The bishop orders his wife to hurry and fetch the candlesticks, while the authorities stand there dumbfounded. They ask, "Are you saying he told us the truth?"

The bishop replies, "Of course. Thank you for bringing him back. I'm very relieved."

The authorities immediately release Valjean, who is shocked by the turn of events, and the bishop thrusts the retrieved candlesticks into Valjean's knapsack.

Once the authorities leave, the bishop drops the heavy bag of silver at Valjean's feet. After peeling away Valjean's hood, which was cloaking his guilty face, the bishop sternly looks him in the eye and orders him, "Don't forget—don't ever forget you've promised to become a new man."

Valjean, trembling, makes the promise and with utter humility asks, "Why are you doing this?"

The bishop places his hands on Valjean's shoulders as an act of blessing and declares, "Jean Valjean, my brother, you no longer belong to evil. With this silver, I've bought your soul. I've ransomed you from fear and hatred. Now I give you back to God."

Elapsed time: Measured from the Columbia Pictures logo, the scene begins at 00:07:37 and goes to 00:09:47.

Content: Rated PG-13 for some violence and language

Citation: *Les Misérables* (Columbia Pictures, 1998), written by Rafael Yglesias (based on the novel *Les Misérables* by Victor Hugo), directed by Bille August

submitted by Melissa Parks, Des Plaines, Illinois

82. REDEMPTION

Toy Story 2

Topic: *You're Valuable*

Texts: *Genesis 1:27; Psalm 139:14; 2 Corinthians 5:16–19; James 2:5*

Keywords: *Adoption; Fatherhood of God; God the Creator; Human Worth; Redemption*

In the movie *Toy Story 2*, the voices of Tom Hanks and Tim Allen once again bring to life the animated heroes Woody and Buzz Lightyear, two action-packed toys owned by a boy named Andy.

The movie begins as Andy prepares for a week at Cowboy Camp. But just before he leaves, Woody's arm tears at the shoulder, so Andy leaves him behind. Feeling lonely and worthless, Woody wonders if he is nearing that time when a boy abandons his favorite toy for the next high-tech fad.

While pondering his worthlessness, Woody sees fellow toys being taken out to the family yard sale. Woody attempts to rescue his friend, but he is spotted by Al, a greedy toy collector. Al, recognizing Woody's incomparable value as an antique, steals him and takes him to Al's Toy Barn, where Woody is met by a cowgirl named Jessie, who is ecstatic at his arrival.

Woody asks Jessie why anyone would make such a fuss over him. Jessie shows Woody a video. He watches in amazement as it dawns on him that the image on the TV screen is his own. He is the original Sheriff Woody, "the rootin'est, tootin'est sheriff in the West," and the star of a popular 1950s TV show, *Woody's Roundup*.

Woody, boggling over his identity, looks around the room filled with lunch boxes, kids' toys, record albums, even a yo-yo that bear his likeness. "Just look at all this," he exclaims.

Jessie responds, "Didn't you know? You're valuable property!"

Elapsed time: Measured from the beginning of the opening credit, the scene in which Woody views the video and sees his own image begins at 00:20:51 and ends at 00:23:23. The scene in which Jessie tells Woody he's valuable begins at 00:26:20 and ends at 00:26:53.

Content: Rated G

Citation: *Toy Story 2* (Disney, 1999), written by Andrew Stanton, Rita Hsiao, Doug Chamberlain, and Chris Webb, directed by John Lasseter

submitted by Clark Cothern, Tecumseh, Michigan

83. REGRET

On the Waterfront

Topic: *Regretting Wasted Opportunities*

Texts: *Psalm 51; Proverbs 1:10–19; Matthew 26:69–75; Mark 14:72; Luke 22:60–62; Philippians 3:13–14*

Keywords: *Attitudes and Emotions; Compromise; Consequences; Crime; Despair; Destiny; Failure; Future; Mistakes; Opportunity; Purpose; Redemption; Regret; Shame; Significance; Sowing and Reaping*

In the 1954 movie *On the Waterfront,* Marlon Brando stars as a former boxer named Terry Malloy. When the movie begins, Malloy's boxing days are long past, and he has been reduced to an errand boy for the mob.

As the movie progresses, we learn that Malloy once had the potential to be a championship prize fighter, but he squandered his opportunity by agreeing to the mob's request that he take a dive in the boxing ring when he could have won the fight easily. Sadly, the encouragement to throw the fight came from his own mobster brother, Charlie (played by Rod Steiger).

The consequences of Terry's choices are numerous. He squanders a promising boxing career and a shot at the title. He becomes entangled with the mob and, unwittingly, a mob hit. When Terry is subpoenaed, the mob sends his brother, Charlie, to convince him to keep his mouth shut. On a ride in the back of a cramped taxi, Charlie begins to chide Terry for squandering his boxing career. Charlie says, "You coulda been another Billy Caan. That skunk we got you for a manager, he brought you along too fast."

Terry stares in disbelief. Looking from beneath eyelids puffy and scarred from boxing, a dumbfounded Terry says, "It wasn't the manager. It was you, Charlie. You remember that night in the Garden you came down and said, 'It's not your night, kid.' It's not your night? I coulda torn Wilson apart!"

The heartbreak of a future that has been lost creases Terry's face. Then all of Terry's regret pours out like a river. "I coulda had class! I coulda been a contender! I coulda been somebody! Instead of a bum, which is what I am."

All the rage of the boxer recedes as quickly as it came and is replaced by the hopeless look of a man who has seen his future slip away.

(Terry eventually redeems himself. He stops looking back over his shoulder at what could have been. He begins making difficult—but good—choices. Terry goes to trial and testifies against the mob and becomes the somebody—the person of class—he wanted to be.)

Elapsed time: Measured from the Columbia Pictures logo, the scene begins at 01:13:42 and ends at 01:15:00.

Content: Not rated—no offensive language, but there are some violent scenes and a sensual scene.

Citation: *On the Waterfront* (Columbia Pictures, 1954), written by Budd Schulberg, directed by Elia Kazan

submitted by David Slagle, Lawrenceville, Georgia

84. SECRETS

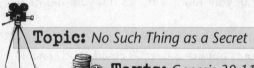

Topic: *No Such Thing as a Secret*

Texts: *Genesis 39:11–23; 2 Samuel 11:1–5;
Matthew 10:26; Mark 4:22; Luke 8:17;
Luke 12:2–3; John 3:19; Romans 2:16;
1 Corinthians 4:5; 1 Corinthians 6:18;
Hebrews 4:13*

Keywords: *Aging; Character; Compromise; Conscience;
Darkness; Deception; Faithfulness; Holiness; Honesty;
Integrity; Light; Lust; Marriage; Men; Middle Age;
Purity; Secrets; Sex; Sexual Immorality; Temptation;
Truth; Unfaithfulness*

The comedy *City Slickers* explores the serious issues men face as
they approach midlife. To get his mind off his approaching for-
tieth birthday, urbanite Mitch Robbins (played by Billy Crystal) talks
two of his city-dwelling friends—who also are on the verge of midlife
crises—to go on a vacation with him. It's not your typical week on
the beach or golf course. They sign up for a cattle drive from New
Mexico to Colorado. All three city slickers hope that the time away
from the ordinary will help them find their way.

Under the big sky of the rural West, Mitch and one of his friends,
Ed (played by Bruno Kirby), are on horseback, attempting to drive a
herd of cattle. With the sounds of cattle mooing in the background,
Ed poses a series of hypothetical situations to see what Mitch would
be willing to do if he knew no one would find out.

Ed first asks Mitch if he'd be unfaithful to his wife if he knew she'd never find out and if the other woman was very attractive. Mitch doesn't take the bait. He says such a situation would most likely be a trap.

Ed persists. "Let's say a spaceship lands, and the most beautiful girl you ever saw gets out. And all she wants is to have the greatest sex in the universe with you."

Mitch is willing to contemplate this unlikely scenario.

Ed continues, "And the second it's over, she flies away for eternity. No one will ever know. You're telling me you wouldn't do it?"

Mitch says that this very scenario actually happened to his cousin, Ronald. Ed isn't humored in the least.

Suddenly Mitch becomes serious. He looks at Ed and confesses, "What I'm saying is that it wouldn't make it all right if Barbara didn't know. I'd know—and I wouldn't like myself."

Elapsed time: Measured from the beginning of the opening credit, this scene begins at 01:29:35 and lasts about one minute.

Content: Rated PG-13 for language and adult situations

Citation: *City Slickers* (Columbia Pictures, 1991), written by Lowell Ganz and Babaloo Mandell, directed by Ron Underwood

submitted by Greg Asimakoupoulos, Naperville, Illinois, and Doug Scott, Elgin, Illinois

85. SEEKING GOD

Contact

Topic: *Searching for God*

Texts: *Psalm 145:18; Jeremiah 29:13; Luke 12:31; John 14:18; Hebrews 11:6*

Keywords: *Belief; Death; Doubt; Faith; Family; Fatherhood of God; Fathers; Loneliness; Orphans; Prayer; Seeking God; Separation; Spiritual Hunger; Unbelief*

Contact is a science-fiction movie that explores the possibility of extraterrestrial life and the inevitability of faith, even in a world governed by scientific logic. The plot follows the career of female astronomer Ellie Arroway. Ellie (played by Jodie Foster) longs for contact with life beyond this world. She is convinced that a universe with life only on earth would be a waste of space.

As a scientist, she dismisses faith in God because of the absence of empirical proof. Ironically, she maintains a belief in aliens, even though she lacks credible evidence. Ellie is transformed, however, when she contacts alien beings. She travels to deep space but cannot convince skeptics that she has done so, because she lacks scientific proof. She finally realizes that not everything that is true can be reduced to test-tube analysis.

Although Ellie's mother died giving birth, Ellie has a remarkable relationship with her dad. He encourages her scientific curiosity and introduces her to long-distance contact through a ham radio. Sadly, when Ellie is nine years old, her father dies of a heart attack. On the day of the funeral, the family pastor attempts to comfort the grief-stricken little girl.

"Ellie," he says, "I know it's hard to understand now, but we aren't always meant to know the reasons why things happen the way they do. Sometimes we just have to accept it as God's will."

Because Ellie feels responsible for not getting her dad's heart medicine to him in time, she is unwilling to accept the minister's counsel. Her searching eyes lock on the minister's caring glance but find no comfort. She retreats to her bedroom.

Feeling desperately alone, Ellie leans forward at her desk in front of her ham radio, painfully calling out for her father in heaven: "Dad? Dad? Are you there? Come back, Dad!" As the extended family members mingle on the main floor of the home, little Ellie slowly repeats her plea: "Dad? Dad? Are you there? Come back, Dad!"

The camera pulls out, revealing a little girl longing for assurance that she is not alone.

Elapsed time: Measured from the beginning of the opening credit, this scene begins at 00:23:09 and lasts approximately two minutes.

Content: Rated PG for sexual content and language

Citation: *Contact* (Warner Brothers, 1997), written by James V. Hart and Michael Goldenberg (based on the novel by Carl Sagan), directed by Robert Zemeckis

submitted by Greg Asimakoupoulos, Naperville, Illinois

86. SELFISHNESS

Rules of Engagement

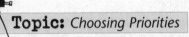

Topic: *Choosing Priorities*

Texts: *Matthew 26:69–75; Mark 14:66–72; Luke 22:54–62; Philippians 2:3–4; 2 Timothy 4:16–17; Revelation 12:11*

Keywords: *Betrayal; Choices; Conflict; Dishonor; Priorities; Selfishness*

Rules of Engagement explores the conflict surrounding a fictional military tragedy. Marine colonel Terry Childers (played by Samuel L. Jackson), leads a team to rescue United States Ambassador Mourain, his wife, and their young son from the American embassy in Yemen, where protesters have become hostile.

Colonel Childers successfully removes the ambassador and his family, but when gunfire erupts and Childers believes the protesters are firing on his men, he gives the order to open fire on the crowd below.

The large loss of apparently civilian life ignites a firestorm that burns all the way up the political ladder to the national security advisor, who, in an effort to deflect blame from the United States, creates a scapegoat by painting Colonel Childers as an overzealous soldier who snapped under pressure. A court martial is quickly convened for the murder of presumably innocent people. Childers is charged with violating "the rules of engagement."

Childers turns to a military lawyer named Colonel Hodges (played by Tommy Lee Jones). Hodges discovers a trail of evidence that leads him to believe that a videotape vindicating his client has been hidden or destroyed. He also believes that Ambassador Mourain has lied under oath to protect his own political reputation, leaving Colonel Childers to take all the blame.

After the first day of testimony, Hodges drives to Mourain's house and personally confronts the ambassador's wife (played by Anne Archer). "Mrs. Mourain, I don't believe your husband is telling the truth about what Colonel Childers did in Yemen. Can you tell me that Colonel Childers . . . kept your husband from doing his duty?"

"No. As far as I'm concerned, he behaved quite honorably."

"Will you testify to that?"

"My husband's a good man," comes her veiled reply.

"So is Colonel Childers."

"I've been married for ten years," she says. "You're asking me to throw all that away in one afternoon."

"You and your husband and your son owe your lives to Colonel Terry Childers."

"We all have our priorities, Colonel," she answers. With that she walks into her house, shutting the door behind her.

Elapsed time: Measured from the movie's first scene, this scene begins at 01:23:18 and goes to 01:23:41.

Content: Rated R for extreme profanity and graphic war violence

Citation: *Rules of Engagement* (Paramount, 2000), written by Stephen Gaghan (based on a story by James Webb), directed by William Friedkin

submitted by Clark Cothern, Tecumseh, Michigan

87. SELFLESSNESS

Princess Diaries

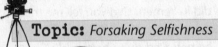

Topic: *Forsaking Selfishness*

Texts: *Matthew 20:20–28; Mark 10:35–45; Philippians 2:1–11*

Keywords: *Sacrifice; Selflessness; Service; Unselfishness*

In the movie *The Princess Diaries*, young princess Mia Thermopolis (played by Anne Hathaway) makes a speech about her decision whether or not to accept the role as princess of Genovia:

"I wondered how I'd feel after abdicating my role as princess of Genovia. Would I feel relieved, or would I feel sad? And then I realized how many stupid times a day I use the word *I*. In fact, probably all I ever do is think about myself. And how lame is that when there are seven billion people out there on this planet? But then I thought, if I cared about the other seven billion people out there instead of just me, that's probably a much better use of my time. You see, if I were princess of Genovia, then my thoughts and the thoughts of people smarter than me would be much better heard—and just maybe those thoughts could be turned into action."

Elapsed time: Measured from the beginning of the video, the scene begins at 01:42:30 and goes to 01:43:45.

Content: Rated G

Citation: *The Princess Diaries* (Disney, 2001), written by Gina Wendkos (based on the novel by Meg Cabot), directed by Garry Marshall

submitted by Mike Thorburn, Nova Scotia, Canada

88. SELF-WORTH

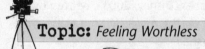

Princess Diaries

Topic: *Feeling Worthless*

Texts: *Matthew 5:1–12; Matthew 9:36; Matthew 23:37; Luke 10:25–37; Luke 14:12–14; Luke 19:41–44; Colossians 3:12*

Keywords: *Human Worth; Self-Image; Self-Worth; Significance*

In the movie *The Princess Diaries*, Mia Thermopolis (played by Anne Hathaway) is a shy, awkward teenager whose only goal in life is to be invisible. She tries to get through each day with as little attention as possible. Her world is turned upside down when her estranged grandmother arrives to tell her that she is a real-life princess. Mia reluctantly decides to take "princess lessons" and to accept her royal position—all in just three weeks. Becoming royalty proves to be more arduous, less glamorous, and ultimately more fulfilling than she thought.

The movie begins with a typical day at Grove High School, with the popular girls flirting with the popular guys. Mia starts off her day, once again feeling lost, left out, and unimportant. She is standing next to her friend Lily and greets a passing teacher with a cheerful "Good morning, Ms. Gupta." Ms. Gupta can't even remember Mia's name and instead responds to Lily, "Good morning, Lily." Then, with an awkward pause, she looks at Mia and adds, "and Lily's friend."

The next scene shows Mia, with books in hand, walking through a crowd and sitting down on a low wall. Without warning, a male student, caught up in conversation and unaware of her, comes over and accidentally sits on her. He quickly apologizes and moves on, but the damage is done. Mia grimly utters to Lily, "Somebody sat on me—again."

Do you ever feel like Mia? Invisible? Sat on?

Elapsed time: Measured from the beginning of the opening credit, this scene begins at 00:00:55 and lasts approximately two minutes.

Content: Rated G

Citation: *Princess Diaries* (Disney, 2001), written by Gina Wendkos (based on the novel by Meg Cabot), directed by Garry Marshall

submitted by Bill White, Paramount, California

89. SERVANTHOOD

First Knight

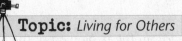

Topic: *Living for Others*

Texts: *Psalm 41:1; Proverbs 3:27–28; Matthew 10:39; Mark 14:6–9; John 13:1–17; Romans 12:7; Philippians 2:3–8; 1 Timothy 6:18; 1 Peter 4:10; 1 John 3:16–18*

Keywords: *Church; Community; Dying to Self; Generosity; Love; Ministry; Purpose; Sacrifice; Selfishness; Self-Reliance; Servanthood; Service; Unselfishness*

In the movie *First Knight,* Lancelot (played by Richard Gere) is a wanderer and a highly skilled swordsman who fights for whomever will pay him. Seeing a princess and her entourage under attack in the woods, he decides to save her. Attracted to the princess Guinevere (played by Julia Ormond), he later visits her in Camelot, where an annual festival is taking place. Unfortunately for him, Guinevere is to be wed to King Arthur (played by Sean Connery) at a later date.

In one particular scene, King Arthur and Camelot's values of serving others and something greater than yourself is contrasted with Lancelot's selfish and solitary lifestyle. Following Lancelot's success at "running the Gauntlet," an impossible obstacle course of swinging boulders and axes, King Arthur meets Lancelot. Arthur is thoroughly impressed with Lancelot's ability to run the Gauntlet, and wants to know how he did it. Lancelot responds that fear caused others to fail, but, "I have nothing to lose, so what have I to fear?" He has no home and no family. Proudly he claims, "I live by my sword."

As they walk toward the room that holds the Round Table, King Arthur tells Lancelot what Camelot's values are: "Here we believe that every life is precious, even the lives of strangers. If you must die, die serving something greater than yourself. Better still, live and serve."

At the Round Table, where the High Council of Camelot meets, King Arthur tells him the table has no head or foot; they are all equal, even the King. Lancelot reads the inscription on the table: "In serving each other we become free."

King Arthur remarks, "That is the very heart of Camelot. Not these stones, timbers, towers, palaces. Burn them all, and Camelot lives on. Because it lives in us, it's a belief we hold in our hearts."

King Arthur invites Lancelot to stay in Camelot, but Lancelot wants to be on the road, wherever chance takes him. As he's leaving, King Arthur tells him, "Lancelot, just a thought. A man who fears nothing is a man who loves nothing. And if you love nothing, what joy is there in your life?"

Elapsed time: Measured from the opening credit, this scene begins at 00:44:20 and ends at 00:47:50.

Content: Rated PG-13 for violent medieval battles

Citation: *First Knight* (Columbia, 1995), written by William Nicholson (based on a story by Lorne Cameron, David Hoselton, and William Nicholson), directed by Jerry Zucker

submitted by Jerry De Luca,
Montreal West, Quebec, Canada

90. SIGNIFICANCE

Requiem for a Heavyweight

Topic: *Our Need for Dignity*

Texts: *Genesis 1:26–28; Psalm 8:4–8;*
Psalm 139:13–16; Matthew 6:26–30;
Romans 8:14–17, 29; 2 Corinthians 3:18;
2 Corinthians 5:17; Ephesians 1:11;
Ephesians 2:10; Philippians 2:12–13;
1 John 3:1–3

Keywords: *Anger; Career; Dignity; Disabilities; Loss;*
Men; Pride; Purpose; Rejection; Self-Worth; Significance;
Sports; Vocation; Weakness; Work

Requiem for a Heavyweight, with Anthony Quinn, Jackie Gleason, and Mickey Rooney, is a 1962 film about a thirty-seven-year-old boxer forced to quit due to head injuries. He must now find something else to do with his life.

In this scene, Mountain Rivera (played by Anthony Quinn) is in an employment office with a woman employment counselor (played by Julie Harris). His face shows the bruises and scars from seventeen years of boxing. His voice is thick and slow from taking too many punches. He explains to the employment counselor that he left school after sixth grade, and the only job he's ever had has been professional fighting.

The counselor says, "You're a prize fighter. It would be rather difficult to place you in any kind of related field."

Rivera responds, "Well, I need a job. So anything you got is okay. You know, uh, dishwashing, maybe a bouncer, or even a day laborer."

"But we have to take into account past experience," the counselor retorts.

Rivera says, "What else am I supposed to know what to do besides fight? That question there—*Why did you leave your last job?* What am I supposed to write down? The doctor said no more. He looked into my eyes and said one or two more and I might go blind. It's just a bum break, that's all. You know, in 1952 they ranked me number five. I'm not kidding you; they ranked me number five! That was no easy year either. There was Marciano, Walcott, and Charleston around, but they had me up there number five . . ."

The counselor interrupts, "Well, as long as we have your address written down here, we'll contact you if anything comes up."

"Yeah, sure, sure, sure, miss"—and Rivera heads for the door with resignation written all over his face.

"Mr. Rivera," the counselor blurts out, "right after the war I did a lot of work with disabled veterans." She pauses. "Well, I meant, I meant you'd be surprised at the different kinds of openings that come up for . . ."

"You mean for cripples and guys like that," interjects Rivera.

The counselor says, "No, I didn't mean just that. I meant for, uh, for people who have special problems."

Rivera has one last thing to say. "Miss, I got no special problem. You know I'm a big ugly slob, and I look like a freak. But I was almost the heavyweight champion of the world! Why don't you put that down on that paper someplace? Mountain Rivera was no punk. Mountain Rivera was almost the heavyweight champion of the world!"

Rivera opens the door and walks out.

Elapsed time: This scene begins at 00:22:50 and goes to 00:28:00.

Content: Not rated

Citation: *Requiem for a Heavyweight* (Columbia Pictures, 1962), written by Rod Serling (based on Serling's 1956 teleplay written for TV's "Playhouse 90"), directed by Ralph Nelson

submitted by Jerry De Luca,
Montreal West, Quebec, Canada

91. SOWING AND REAPING

Mr. Holland's Opus

Topic: *Leaving a Legacy*

Texts: *2 Corinthians 3:1–3; Ephesians 5:27; Philippians 4:1; 1 Thessalonians 2:19–20; 1 Timothy 4:12*

Keywords: *Ambition; Career; Discipleship; Fame; Family; Fruit; Fruitfulness; Frustration; Goals; Harvest; Leadership; Legacy; Mentoring; Ministry; Mission; Pastors; Relationships; Results; Sowing and Reaping; Success; Teachers; Teenagers; Work; Youth*

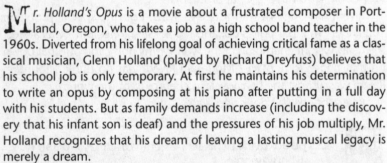

Mr. Holland's Opus is a movie about a frustrated composer in Portland, Oregon, who takes a job as a high school band teacher in the 1960s. Diverted from his lifelong goal of achieving critical fame as a classical musician, Glenn Holland (played by Richard Dreyfuss) believes that his school job is only temporary. At first he maintains his determination to write an opus by composing at his piano after putting in a full day with his students. But as family demands increase (including the discovery that his infant son is deaf) and the pressures of his job multiply, Mr. Holland recognizes that his dream of leaving a lasting musical legacy is merely a dream.

At the end of the movie we find an aged Mr. Holland fighting in vain to keep his job. The board has decided to reduce the operating budget by cutting the music and drama program. No longer a reluctant band teacher, Mr. Holland believes in what he does and passionately defends the role of the arts in public education. What began as a career detour became a thirty-five-year mission, pouring his heart into the lives of young people.

Mr. Holland returns to his classroom to retrieve his belongings a few days after school has let out for summer vacation. He has taught his final class. With regret and sorrow, he fills a box with artifacts that represent the tools of his trade and memories of many meaningful classes. His wife and son arrive to give him a hand.

As they leave the room and walk down the hall, Mr. Holland hears some noise in the auditorium. Because school is out, he opens the door to see what the commotion is all about. To his amazement he sees a capacity audience of former students and teaching colleagues and a banner that reads "Good-bye, Mr. Holland." Those in attendance greet Mr. Holland with a standing ovation, while a band (consisting of past and present members) plays songs they learned at his hand.

His wife, who was in on the surprise reception, approaches the podium and makes small talk until the master of ceremonies—the governor of Oregon—arrives. The governor is none other than a student Mr. Holland helped to believe in herself his first year of teaching. As she addresses the room of well-wishers, she speaks for the hundreds who fill the auditorium:

"Mr. Holland had a profound influence in my life (on a lot of lives, I know), and yet I get the feeling that he considers a great part of his life misspent. Rumor had it he was always working on this symphony of his, and this was going to make him famous and rich (probably both). But Mr. Holland isn't rich, and he isn't famous—at least not outside our little town. So it might be easy for him to think himself a failure, but he'd be wrong. Because I think he's achieved a success far beyond riches and fame."

Looking at her former teacher, the governor gestures with a sweeping hand and continues, "Look around you. There is not a life in this room that you have not touched, and each one of us is a better person because of you. We are your symphony, Mr. Holland. We are the melodies and the notes of your opus. And we are the music of your life."

Elapsed time: Measured from the beginning of the opening credit, this scene begins at 02:05:50 and lasts about five minutes.

Content: Rated PG for mild profanity

Citation: *Mr. Holland's Opus* (Hollywood Pictures, 1995), written by Patrick Sheane Duncan, directed by Stephen Herek

submitted by Greg Asimakoupoulos, Naperville, Illinois

92. STRENGTH

Ruby Bridges

Topic: *Grace under Pressure*

Texts: *Psalm 112:7–8; Proverbs 3:5–6; Matthew 5:44; John 16:33; Acts 7:60; Romans 12:14; 1 Corinthians 16:13; Philippians 1:20; 2 Timothy 3:12; 1 Peter 4:12–13*

Keywords: *Adversity; Children; Courage; Faith; Family; Grace; Love for Enemies; Persecution; Perseverance; Prayer; Prayer for Enemies; Pressure; Purpose; Strength; Stress; Trials*

Ruby Bridges tells the true story of the six-year-old girl who became the first person of color in the United States to attend, by federal law, an all-white school in 1960-segregationist New Orleans, Louisiana. Ruby faced overwhelming social adversity.

As the scene starts, Ruby (played by Chaz Monet) is walking through the angry crowd outside the school with four federal agents around her. As she goes up the steps, she suddenly turns around, walks down a few steps, stops, and appears to say something to the crowd. The agents try to coax her back up the steps. She resists for a moment, her lips still moving. A psychiatrist (an expert in child stress who had offered the family free counseling) is there looking on. Ruby then turns around and is escorted into the school.

In the next scene, Ruby and the psychiatrist (played by Kevin Pollak) are sitting alone at the family's kitchen table. She is coloring. He says, "But honey, I saw you talking to them. Did you finally get angry with them? Did you tell them to just leave you alone?"

Ruby answers, "No. I didn't tell them anything. I didn't talk to them."

"But Ruby, I was there. I saw your lips moving."

"I wasn't talking to them. I was praying for them."

The doctor is startled. "Praying for them?"

"Yes, I pray for them every day in the car. But I forgot that day."

"Oh. What prayer did you say?"

Ruby puts down her crayon, folds her hands together, and says, "Please God, forgive these people, because even if they say these mean things, they don't know what they're doing, so you can forgive them, just like you did those folks a long time ago when they said terrible things about you."

The doctor, deeply moved, closes his eyes momentarily.

In the next scene, the whole family is together in the living room, along with the doctor and his wife. The father expresses his appreciation to the doctor, saying that all his attention is helping Ruby feel special. The doctor says, "I appreciate your kind words very much, but I think what makes Ruby feel so special is you and your family—and something greater than all of us. All this time I've wondered what makes her so strong."

In the next scene, the doctor's wife is at her typewriter, listening to a big 1960-style tape recorder, and typing her husband's words: "And so I learned that a family and a child under great stress and fear can show exquisite dignity and courage because of their moral and religious values. They had a definite purpose in what they were trying to accomplish. This purpose made them resilient. I couldn't figure out the source of the resilience because I only worked with well-to-do children who really had nothing to work hard for. No reason driving them to accomplish anything. So now I see that the issue is not stress, but stress for what purpose? Having something to believe in protected Ruby from psychiatric symptoms and gave her a dignity and a strength that is utterly remarkable."

As we hear this, there is a silent scene of Ruby reading out loud in class while a white boy sticks his fingers in his ears. She looks at him with only mild annoyance.

Elapsed time: Measured from the beginning of the opening credit, these scenes begin at 01:11:53 and end at 01:16:18.

Content: Not rated

Citation: *Ruby Bridges* (Disney, 1998), written by Toni Ann Johnson, directed by Euzhan Palcy

submitted by Jerry De Luca, Montreal West, Quebec, Canada

93. SUCCESS

Field of Dreams

Topic: *Choosing Priorities*

Texts: *Joshua 24:15; Matthew 16:24–28;*
Matthew 22:37–38; Luke 14:28–33;
2 Corinthians 6:1–2; Philippians 3:1–14

Keywords: *Aging; Choices; Decisions; Desire; Dreams;*
Failure; Goals; Guidance; Hope; Loss; Opportunity;
Priorities; Quitting; Success; Vocation; Wisdom; Work

Field of Dreams is a movie about baseball, pursuing a dream, and choosing life's priorities. Halfway through the film, Ray Kinsella (played by Kevin Costner) travels back in time to meet with Doc Graham (played by Burt Lancaster). Doc had been a rookie ballplayer who made it to the big leagues for one season only to play for half an inning—never making a defensive play, never getting to bat.

The two men walk into Doc's office, speaking wistfully about the joy and beauty of the game of baseball, the smell of leather, and the sound of the crowd. Yet, after his half inning on the brink of glory, Doc had walked away from baseball, choosing to live out the rest of his days doctoring in his hometown. His chief regret: If only he could have gotten to bat, just once, he would have stood strong at the plate, looked the pitcher right in the eye—and winked. How he would have enjoyed that! Just once.

Yet he walked away. Why? "I couldn't bear the thought of another year in the minors," says Doc. "So I decided to hang 'em up."

"What was that like?" Ray asks.

"It was like coming this close to your dreams and watching them brush past you like a stranger in a crowd. At the time you don't think much of it. We just don't recognize the most significant moments of our lives while they're happening. Back then I thought, *Well, there will be other days.* I didn't realize—that was the only day."

"Fifty years ago you came so close," says Ray. "It would kill some men to get that close to their dream and not touch it. They'd consider it a tragedy."

"Son, if I'd only gotten to be a doctor for half an inning, now *that* would have been a tragedy."

Elapsed time: Measured from the initial flashing of the studio symbol, this scene begins at 01:04:05 and ends at 01:09:30.

Content: Rated PG—a family-oriented film that conveys the value of family life, doing what's right, and reconciling differences in family relationships. However, there is a reference in the opening scene to marijuana usage, as well as a few occasions of mildly offensive language.

Citation: *Field of Dreams* (Universal Pictures, 1989), written and directed by Phil Alden Robinson (based on the novel *Shoeless Joe* by W. P. Kinsella)

submitted by Gary Wilde

94. TEMPTATION

It's a Wonderful Life

Topic: *Resisting Temptation*

Texts: *Psalm 146; Amos 6:4–7; Matthew 4:1–11; Luke 4:1–13; Luke 16:19–31; Ephesians 6:10–18; 1 Timothy 6:6–19; James 1:1–8; 1 Peter 5:8–11*

Keywords: *Courage; Evil; Faithfulness; Greed; Integrity; Money; Satan; Seduction; Temptation*

The classic film *It's a Wonderful Life* celebrates George Bailey's contribution to his community. George (played by Jimmy Stewart) is a generous and compassionate proprietor of a local building and loan institution.

George offers loans to individuals denied by the bank headed by the greedy Mr. Potter (played by Lionel Barrymore). George helps countless young families move out of Potter-owned rentals and buy their own homes. Threatened by George and his loan company, Mr. Potter invites George to join his company. George sits in Mr. Potter's ornately carved chair, a symbol of Potter's success. A blazing fire roars in the fireplace, and the old miser sits in a wheelchair positioned in front of a massive desk. After offering George an expensive cigar, Potter paints a picture of the struggling life this young twenty-eight-year-old man, George Bailey, must have: a young wife, family needs, a business that is always struggling, and a salary of $40 a week.

"What's your point, Mr. Potter?" George asks.

"My point is I want to hire you," Potter responds. "I want you to manage my affairs and run my properties. George, I'll start you at $20,000 a year."

Shocked, George drops his lit cigar in his lap, and his eyes double in size. "Twenty thousand dollars a year?" he asks in disbelief.

"You wouldn't mind living in the nicest house in town, buying your wife a lot of fine clothes, a couple business trips to New York a year—maybe once in a while Europe. You wouldn't mind that, would you, George?"

Looking over his shoulder, George asks, "You're not talking to someone else, are you? This is me, George Bailey."

"I know who you are. George Bailey—whose ship has just come in, providing he has enough brains to climb aboard."

George is enticed by the promise of materialistic security, though it would mean relinquishing his family business. Potter agrees to let George sleep on the decision for twenty-four hours and holds out his hand. George grips the hand but then pulls back, coming to his senses.

"I don't need twenty-four hours. I know right now the answer is no. You sit around here and you spin your little web, and you think the world revolves around you and your money. Well, it doesn't, Mr. Potter. In the whole vast configuration of things, I'd say you were nothing but a scurvy little spider."

Elapsed time: Measured from the beginning of the opening credit, this scene begins at 01:07:02 and lasts approximately five minutes.

Content: Rated G

Citation: *It's a Wonderful Life* (Liberty Films/RKO Radio Pictures, 1946), written by Frances Goodrich, Albert Hackett, Jo Swerling, and Frank Capra (based on "The Greatest Gift," a short story written by Philip Van Doren Stern), directed by Frank Capra

submitted by Greg Asimakoupoulos, Naperville, Illinois

95. TEMPTATION

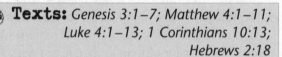

The Lion King

Topic: *Power of Temptation*

Texts: *Genesis 3:1–7; Matthew 4:1–11;*
Luke 4:1–13; 1 Corinthians 10:13;
Hebrews 2:18

Keywords: *Devil; Satan; Sin; Temptation*

Disney's animated film *The Lion King* portrays the struggle between good and evil through the adventures of a lion named Simba. Simba, the son of Mufasa, the lion king, faces challenges while assuming his rightful inheritance. Through trials he finds his purpose in life.

In one scene, Simba talks with Scar, his jealous uncle. The young cub is filled with excitement about someday becoming king. Unaware of Scar's desire to usurp the throne, Simba boasts, "Hey, Uncle Scar. Guess what. I'm going to be king of Pride Rock."

"Oh, goodie," says Scar.

"My dad just showed me the whole kingdom," Simba continues, "and I'm going to rule it all."

"So your father showed you the whole kingdom, did he?" Scar asks. He motions to a shadowy land on the horizon and says, "He didn't show you what's beyond that rise on the northern border."

"Well, no," Simba admits. "He said I can't go there."

"And he's absolutely right," Scar says. "It's too dangerous. Only the bravest lions go there."

"Well, I'm brave," little Simba says. "What's out there?"

"Oh, I'm sorry, Simba," says Uncle Scar. "I just can't tell you. I'm only looking out for the well-being of my favorite nephew.... An elephant graveyard is no place for a young prince. Promise me you'll never visit that dreadful place."

Scar feigns innocence at divulging the location of the forbidden territory. He apologizes—but knows he has succeeded in awakening Simba's will to disobey his father.

As the young cub leaves his uncle, he seeks out his playmate, Nala, with whom he goes to explore the banned elephant graveyard. They are surprised by evil hyenas and barely escape.

Elapsed time: Measured from the beginning of the opening credit, this scene begins at 00:11:06 and lasts approximately two minutes.

Content: Rated G

Citation: *The Lion King* (Disney, 1994), written by Jim Capobianco, Irene Mecchi, Jonathan Roberts, and Linda Woolverton, directed by Roger Allers and Rob Minkoff

submitted by Greg Asimakoupoulos, Naperville, Illinois

96. TEMPTATION

Pinocchio

Topic: *Imprisoning Power of Sin*

Texts: *Genesis 3:1–7; John 8:44; Romans 6:11–14; Romans 7:14; James 1:13–15*

Keywords: *Ambition; Bondage; Deception; Fame; Satan; Sin; Slavery; Temptation*

Pinocchio is based on the nineteenth-century children's story by Carlo Collodi. An old woodcarver named Geppetto lives alone with a pet cat and a goldfish in the European Alps. One day he carves a little boy puppet and names him Pinocchio. Whenever he sees the marionette, he thinks how wonderful it would be to have a real son.

As he views the wishing star in the sky, Geppetto wishes that Pinocchio would become real. During the night the Blue Fairy brings the puppet to life, removes his strings, and instructs the little wooden boy to shun evil and follow good. She provides him with a cricket by the name of Jiminy to be his conscience.

One day Pinocchio is diverted from going to school by a couple of conniving characters who tempt him to seek a life of fame and fortune as an actor. They recognize the commercial value of a puppet who can walk and talk. They introduce Pinocchio to a carnival operator by the name of Stromboli. Pinocchio becomes the star of Stromboli's marionette show and generates lots of money.

In this scene the carnival operator sings loudly as he counts his money in a back room. Pinocchio naively looks on.

"Bravo, Pinocchio!" Stromboli cheers.

"They liked me!" Pinocchio says.

Stromboli says, "You were sensational. You were colossal."

"Does that mean I'm an actor?" Pinocchio asks.

"Sure. I will push you in the public's eye. Your face will be on everybody's tongue."

Stromboli's greedy visions of how much his wooden slave will earn him are interrupted as he detects a counterfeit coin in his pile of earnings. Irritated, he tosses the worthless piece to Pinocchio, suggesting that it is his wage. The boy does not realize he is being taken advantage of and announces that he wants to run home and show his father his income.

Stromboli grabs him and locks him in a cage. "This will be your home," he says.

He gathers all his gold coins together and makes it clear that Pinocchio is not free any longer. "To me you are belonging," he says. "We will tour the world together. . . . You will make lots of money for me. And when you are growing too old, you will make good firewood." Stromboli throws the ax he has been holding into a pile of old wooden toys.

Pinocchio calls out for help, but Stromboli disregards his pleas. He commands his little wooden gold mine to shut up. And then with evil laughter, he leaves the room. Pinocchio realizes that he has become a prisoner.

Elapsed time: Measured from the beginning of the opening credit, this scene begins at 00:40:50 and ends at 00:44:00.

Content: Rated G

Citation: *Pinocchio* (Disney, 1940), written by Aurelius Battaglia, William Cottrell, Otto Englander, Erdman Penner, Joseph Sabo, Ted Sears, and Webb Smith (based on the novel *The Adventures of Pinocchio* by Carlo Collodi), directed by Hamilton Luske and Ben Sharpsteen

submitted by Greg Asimakoupoulos, Naperville, Illinois

97. TRANSFORMATION

As Good as It Gets

Topic: *Love Motivates Change*

Texts: *Luke 19:1–10; John 14:24*

Keywords: *Grace; Growth; Love; Motivation; Obedience; Repentance; Sanctification; Spiritual Formation; Transformation*

A s *Good as It Gets* is a 1997 comedy about three very different people whose lives become entangled. The threesome includes an obsessive-compulsive author, an out-of-work artist, and a struggling waitress. Jack Nicholson plays Melvin Udall, the crude, obsessive-compulsive author. He offends everyone he meets. For example, the movie opens with Melvin tossing a neighbor's pet down the laundry chute of the exclusive apartment building where he lives.

But Melvin becomes enamored with Carol Connelly, a waitress played by Helen Hunt. She has seen him at his worst, but she reluctantly agrees to meet Melvin at a fancy restaurant for a date. Carol arrives at the restaurant and is obviously ill at ease as waiters follow her about and wait on her hand and foot. While the other patrons of the restaurant are impeccably dressed, Carol wears a simple red dress.

Melvin sees Carol at the bar and waves her over to his table. When she approaches, Melvin hits an all-time low. "This restaurant!" he says. "They make me buy a new outfit and let you in wearing a housedress." Carol is stunned and hurt. Yet she doesn't leave.

Carol looks Melvin in the eye and says, "Pay me a compliment, Melvin. I need one—now."

Melvin responds, "I've got a great compliment." *What can he possibly say to undo the thoughtless comment he had just delivered?*

Melvin then delivers one of the most romantic lines in big-screen history. This deeply flawed man, his own worst enemy, looks at Carol with all the kindness and sincerity his shriveled heart can muster and says, "Carol, you make me want to be a better man."

Elapsed time: Measured from the opening credit, this scene begins at 01:37:15 and ends at 01:40:38.

Content: Rated PG-13 for language and some sexual content

Citation: *As Good as It Gets* (Tristar Pictures, 1997), written by Mark Andrus and James L. Brooks, directed by James L. Brooks

submitted by David Slagle, Lawrenceville, Georgia

98. TRIALS

Snow Dogs

Topic: *When Everything Goes Wrong*

Texts: *Psalm 119:82, 107; Isaiah 38:4–6; Jonah 2;
Matthew 15:22–28; Luke 18:1; James 5:13–16*

Keywords: *Adversity; Despair; Desperation; Difficulties;
Help from God; Problems; Silence; Trials; Unanswered
Prayer*

Snow Dogs is the 2001 Disney movie about a dentist named Ted Brooks (played by Cuba Gooding Jr.) who discovers that he has inherited a rustic cabin and a dogsled team in Alaska.

His efforts to master the new sport meet with bumps, bruises, and bears. One particular outing proves especially challenging. When the dogs suddenly go into high gear, Brooks is thrown into the deep Alaskan snow. He struggles to his feet, growling and dusting the snow off. As a large shadow covers his own, he realizes that he's not the only one growling. A large grizzly bear is only a few feet away. When the bear roars, displaying a full set of sharp teeth, Brooks begins to run down the mountainside.

Just as it appears that the bear will win the race, Brooks falls off a cliff and lands on a precipice. While he shouts victoriously, "I'm alive! I'm alive!" the precipice gives way, dropping Brooks to a steep slope, where he rockets down the mountain like a bobsled, narrowly missing tree after tree. He screams all the way down until he finally comes to a halt.

He smiles, but his smile quickly fades when he realizes that he's lying on a thin layer of ice covering a lake. As the ice begins to crack beneath him, he lunges forward, leaving a trail of ice water in his wake. Brooks lands on what appears to be a solid piece of floating ice. The ice supports him only momentarily, and Brooks begins to sink.

Brooks reaches for his cell phone and dials 911, only to hear a recorded message: "You are outside of your coverage area. Should you like to expand your service plan, please call back during our business hours."

Elapsed time: Measured from the Disney logo, this scene begins at 00:54:30 and ends at 00:58:20.

Content: Rated PG for mild crude humor

Citation: *Snow Dogs* (Disney, 2001), written by Jim Kouf, Tommy Swerdlow, Michael Goldberg, Mark Gibson, and Philip Halprin (loosely based on Gary Paulsen's book *Winterdance*), directed by Brian Levant

submitted by David Slagle, Lawrenceville, Georgia

99. TRUTH

Yentl

Topic: *Thirsting for Sacred Wisdom*

Texts: *Psalm 1:1–3; Psalm 42:1–2; Isaiah 55:1–3; John 4:6–29; John 6:35; John 7:37–39; Romans 11:33; 1 Corinthians 2:6–16; 1 Peter 2:2–3; 2 Peter 1:5–6*

Keywords: *Curiosity; Knowledge; Learning; Mind; Mystery; Pursuing God; Questions; Spiritual Desire; Spiritual Hunger; Spiritual Thirst; Truth; Wisdom; Women*

Among Eastern European Jews in the early 1900s, the world of sacred and scholarly learning belonged only to men. A young unmarried woman named Yentl (played by Barbra Streisand) has such an insatiable appetite for learning and sacred wisdom that she leaves home, changes her name, masquerades as an older boy, and gets accepted into a Talmudic Academy.

This scene occurs near the beginning of the movie. Yentl is in a Jewish outdoor market selecting a book from a book wagon. The bookseller (played by Jack Lynn) finishes with another customer and addresses Yentl. "You're in the wrong place, miss. Books for women are over here."

Yentl says, "I'd like to buy this one, please."

Taking the book from her, the bookseller responds, "Sacred books are for men!"

"Why?"

"It's the law, that's why."

"Where's it written?"

"Never mind where. It's a law."

"Well, if it's a law, it must be written somewhere. Maybe in here. I'll take it." Yentl grabs for the book.

The bookseller immediately grabs the book back. "Miss, do me a favor. Do yourself a favor." He picks out another book and says, "Oh, here, a nice picture book. Girls like picture books."

Yentl retorts, "What if I told you it's for my father?"

"Why didn't you say?" replies the bookseller, and he puts back the picture book and sells her the book she wants.

In the next scene, Yentl is in the kitchen reading a thick book and cooking a fish on the stove. Her father (played by Nehemiah Persoff) is in an adjoining room tutoring a student in the Talmud. He asks the student questions, and Yentl quickly answers them out loud from the kitchen.

Her father addresses the student. "Who is strong?"

"He who controls his passions," yells Yentl. Yentl's father ignores her. "Concentrate. Try, David," urges Yentl's father.

"He who controls his passions," repeats Yentl from the kitchen.

The student interjects, "I'm trying. He who . . ."

Yentl interrupts, yelling out in a frustrated tone, "He who controls his passions!"

Expressing amazement, the student says, "Yentl knows Talmud?"

"I think that's enough for today," responds the father.

In the next scene, over a game of chess, Yentl tells her father she envies students of the Talmud. They discuss life and the mysteries of the universe while "I'm learning to tell a herring from a carp!"

He tells her that men and women have different obligations "and don't ask why." He gives in to Yentl's requests for another study session. Yentl is happy as she gets a large book from a well-stocked bookshelf. The father tells her to close the shutters.

As she does so she asks, "If you don't have to hide studying from God, then why from the neighbors?"

"Why? Because I trust *God* will understand. I'm not so sure about the neighbors." He reflects on her desire for learning: "Questions, questions. Even when you were little. Does a goat have a soul? What was before the universe?"

They laugh together, but the father is very tired and goes to bed. Yentl, alone, takes a prayer shawl and puts it above her head in front of a bright lamp. Her upper body is mystically silhouetted as she prays, "God, O merciful Father, I'm wrapped in a robe of light, clothed in your glory, that spreads its wings over my soul. May I be worthy."

Elapsed time: Measured from the opening credit, these scenes begin at 00:04:00 and go to 00:10:00.

Content: Rated PG

Citation: *Yentl* (MGM/United Artists, 1983), written by Jack Rosenthal and Barbra Streisand (based on the short story "Yentl the Yeshiva Boy" by Isaac Bashevis Singer), directed by Barbra Streisand

submitted by Jerry De Luca, Montreal West, Quebec, Canada

100. UNBELIEF

The Red Planet

Topic: *Trusting a Ph.D. over God*

Texts: *Psalm 14:1; Psalm 118:5–9; Proverbs 3:5; John 20:24–31; Romans 1:20–32; 1 Corinthians 1:18–31; Hebrews 11:1–3*

Keywords: *Belief; Faith; God the Creator; Mystery; Science; Skepticism; Trust; Unbelief*

The Red Planet is a movie about scientists who attempt to make Mars inhabitable when the planet Earth suffers uncontrollable pollution. Robby Gallagher (played by Val Kilmer) is a mechanical systems engineer who travels to the red planet to update efforts to plant oxygen-producing algae as a prelude to colonization. After being hit by a solar flare while orbiting Mars, most of the crew crash-lands on the surface in an escape pod, leaving only Commander Bowman (played by Carrie-Anne Moss) on board the mother ship. On the surface of Mars, the others make a surprising discovery. Although there is no sign of the previously planted algae, the atmosphere is inexplicably breathable. Gallagher and another crew member, a bioengineer named Dr. Quinn Burchenal (Tom Sizemore), rest on the rocky surface and reflect on the mysteries they've encountered.

Gallagher ponders, "You just can't get around it, can you?"

Equally dumbfounded, Burchenal responds, "I still can't figure out this algae and oxygen business."

"You hate not knowing, don't you?" questions Gallagher.

Sure of his scientific prowess, Burchenal retorts, "Oh, give it time. Believe me, I'll know."

"Yeah, maybe," Gallagher agrees halfheartedly, "but maybe life's just more mysterious than you think it is."

Burchenal jokingly states, "If you want to take the God route—the easy way—that's up to you."

Gallagher questions, "The easy way? There's nothing easy about a spiritual life. It's a lot more difficult than just being intelligent."

Always the scientist, Burchenal replies, "I think you're just ignoring the facts."

"The facts!" Gallagher explodes. "I'll bet you're no fun at Christmas. I'll bet your mom told you there was no tooth fairy when you were four."

"I'm a geneticist," Burchenal reminds him. "I write code, okay? A, G, T, P in different combinations; hacking the human genome, okay? I choose what I choose. Either your kidneys work or you grow six fingers. I do that. Now when you spot God, you let me know. Until then, I'll trust my Ph.D.'s."

Elapsed time: Measured from the beginning of the opening credit, this scene begins at 01:02:30 and ends at 01:03:40.

Content: Rated PG-13 for violence, language, and brief nudity

Citation: *The Red Planet* (Warner Brothers, 2000), written by Chuck Pfarrer and Jonathan Lemkin, directed by Antony Hoffman

submitted by Stephen Nordbye, Charlton, Massachusetts

101. WRESTLING WITH GOD

The Apostle

Topic: *Honest Prayer*

Texts: *Psalm 10; Psalm 13; Philippians 4:6–7; Hebrews 4:14–16*

Keywords: *Anger; Earnestness in Prayer; Honesty; Prayer; Wrestling with God*

The Apostle is a movie about Euliss "Sonny" Dewey (played by Robert Duvall), an energetic minister leading a large ministry in Texas. When he finds out that his wife is having an affair with another minister and that they have stolen his ministry from underneath him, he erupts in anger and bludgeons his wife's lover to death with a baseball bat. Forced to flee town, he resumes ministry in a rural community, where he tries to make sense of his life and his calling as a preacher.

Early in the film, facing the loss of his wife and church, Sonny goes to God in prayer. On a stormy night he paces in his room and raises his voice to heaven. His honest prayer, reminiscent of Job and some of the psalms, conveys his anger and pain to God:

"Somebody, I say, somebody has taken my wife; they've stolen my church! That's the temple I built for you! I'm gonna yell at you 'cause I'm mad at you! I can't take it!

"Give me a sign or somethin'. Blow this pain out of me. Give it to me tonight, Lord God Jehovah. If you won't give me back my wife, give me peace. Give it to me, give it to me, give it to me, give it to me. Give me peace. Give me peace.

212

"I don't know who's been foolin' with me—you or the Devil. I don't know. And I won't even bring the human into this—he's just a mutt—so I'm not even gonna bring him into it. But I'm confused. I'm mad. I love you, Lord, I love you, but I'm mad at you. I am mad at you!

"So deliver me tonight, Lord. What should I do? Now tell me. Should I lay hands on myself? What should I do? I know I'm a sinner and once in a while a womanizer, but I'm your servant! Ever since I was a little boy and you brought me back from the dead, I'm your servant! What should I do? Tell me. I've always called you Jesus; you've always called me Sonny. What should I do, Jesus? This is Sonny talkin' now."

Elapsed time: Measured from the beginning of the opening credit, this scene begins at 00:25:15 and lasts approximately one and one-half minutes.

Content: Rated PG-13 for language and violence

Citation: *The Apostle* (Universal, 1997), written and directed by Robert Duvall

submitted by Bill White, Paramount, California

Scripture Index

Old Testament

Genesis

Genesis 1:26–28	190
Genesis 1:27	174
Genesis 2:18	132
Genesis 3:1–5	116
Genesis 3:1–7	200, 202
Genesis 4:1–12	170
Genesis 39:11–23	178

Exodus

Exodus 4:11	160
Exodus 14:29–17:16	34
Exodus 20:1–17	50
Exodus 20:12	90
Exodus 20:14	14, 86
Exodus 20:16	114
Exodus 22:21	164

Numbers

Numbers 32:23	50

Deuteronomy

Deuteronomy 5:18	14, 86
Deuteronomy 6:4–7	146
Deuteronomy 18:10–14	82
Deuteronomy 30:19	108
Deuteronomy 31:3–8	34
Deuteronomy 31:6	64

Joshua

Joshua 24:14–15	54
Joshua 24:15	108, 196

1 Samuel

1 Samuel 12:15	154
1 Samuel 13:13–14	154
1 Samuel 15:10–29	154
1 Samuel 17:33–37	34

2 Samuel

2 Samuel 11–12	14
2 Samuel 11:1–5	178

2 Kings

2 Kings 2:1–14	138

2 Chronicles

2 Chronicles 16:9	128
2 Chronicles 19:6–7	112

Job

Job 6:8	68
Job 6:20	68
Job 30:26	68

Psalms

Psalm 1:1–3	208
Psalm 2:7	88
Psalm 5:1–3	158
Psalm 8	162

Psalm 8:4–8	190
Psalm 8:5	30
Psalm 10	212
Psalm 13	212
Psalm 14:1	210
Psalm 15:2–5	114
Psalm 16	70
Psalm 18	150
Psalm 19	80
Psalm 22	148
Psalm 22:5	68
Psalm 23	28
Psalm 30:2	28
Psalm 31:24	68, 78
Psalm 32:10	84
Psalm 33:18–19	84
Psalm 38:15	78
Psalm 38:18	114
Psalm 39:11	66
Psalm 41:1	188
Psalm 42:1–2	208
Psalm 43	100
Psalm 51	176
Psalm 51:3–10	48
Psalm 68:5	88
Psalm 68:6	42
Psalm 78:18–22	104
Psalm 84	84
Psalm 107	104
Psalm 112:5	96, 98
Psalm 112:7–8	194
Psalm 118:5	46
Psalm 118:5–9	210
Psalm 119:71	66
Psalm 119:82, 107	206
Psalm 127:3–5	146
Psalm 130:7	78
Psalm 139:13–16	162, 190
Psalm 139:14	174

Psalm 145:18	180
Psalm 146	198

Proverbs

Proverbs 1:10–19	176
Proverbs 3:5	84, 210
Proverbs 3:5–6	194
Proverbs 3:11–12	66
Proverbs 3:27–28	188
Proverbs 5	86
Proverbs 5:18–19	136
Proverbs 6:23–25	86
Proverbs 6:27–29	14
Proverbs 10:9	116
Proverbs 11:24	96, 98
Proverbs 11:28	66
Proverbs 13:12	68
Proverbs 14:12	50
Proverbs 17:17	40, 42
Proverbs 22:9	96
Proverbs 27:17	138
Proverbs 28:1	48

Ecclesiastes

Ecclesiastes 1:1–11	162
Ecclesiastes 2:10–11	50
Ecclesiastes 3:9–14	30
Ecclesiastes 4:9–12	40, 42
Ecclesiastes 5:4–7	54

Isaiah

Isaiah 1:10–18	32
Isaiah 1:11–17	54
Isaiah 9:6	38
Isaiah 30:1	154
Isaiah 38:4–6	206
Isaiah 40:28–31	52
Isaiah 43:1	12
Isaiah 43:1–3	64
Isaiah 44:5	12
Isaiah 45:7–10	160

Isaiah 55:1–3	208
Isaiah 55:11	26
Isaiah 61:3	106
Isaiah 64:8	88

Jeremiah
Jeremiah 17:7	78, 84
Jeremiah 29:11	64, 108, 160
Jeremiah 29:13	180
Jeremiah 39:18	84

Lamentations
| Lamentations 3:38 | 160 |

Joel
| Joel 3:16 | 78 |

Amos
| Amos 5:15 | 112 |
| Amos 6:4–7 | 198 |

Jonah
| Jonah 2 | 206 |

Zechariah
| Zechariah 10:2 | 82 |

Malachi
| Malachi 2:13–16 | 14 |

New Testament

Matthew
Matthew 4:1–11	86, 116, 198, 200
Matthew 4:23–24	28
Matthew 5:1–12	186
Matthew 5:12	106
Matthew 5:21–24	170
Matthew 5:25	20
Matthew 5:27–28	14
Matthew 5:44	194
Matthew 6:7–8	158
Matthew 6:8–9	88
Matthew 6:14–15	170
Matthew 6:26–30	162, 190
Matthew 7:1–5	170
Matthew 7:7–8	104
Matthew 9:36	186
Matthew 10:8	96, 98, 102
Matthew 10:22	56
Matthew 10:26	178
Matthew 10:28	22
Matthew 10:31	162
Matthew 10:39	188
Matthew 12:7	142
Matthew 12:12	162
Matthew 13:20–21	54
Matthew 14:25–32	60, 92
Matthew 15:22–28	206
Matthew 16:24–28	196
Matthew 16:26	110, 118
Matthew 19:4–9	14
Matthew 19:16–22	74
Matthew 19:21	96, 98
Matthew 20:20–28	184
Matthew 20:25–28	124
Matthew 21:21–22	84
Matthew 21:28–32	54
Matthew 22:37–38	196
Matthew 22:37–40	132
Matthew 23:37	186
Matthew 24:5	82
Matthew 25:14–30	16
Matthew 25:34–45	54
Matthew 26:69–75	176, 182
Matthew 28:18–20	16
Matthew 28:19	24
Matthew 28:19–20	34, 110

Mark
| Mark 4:22 | 178 |
| Mark 8:35–37 | 110 |

Mark 9:23   84
Mark 9:50   170
Mark 10:21   96, 98
Mark 10:35–45   184
Mark 11:23–24   84
Mark 14:6–9   188
Mark 14:66–72   82
Mark 14:72   176
Mark 16:16   24

Luke

Luke 1:50   140
Luke 3:11   96, 98
Luke 4:1–13   116, 198, 200
Luke 4:18   72
Luke 6:27–36   172
Luke 6:35–37   122
Luke 6:38   96, 98, 106
Luke 7:50   84
Luke 8:15   62
Luke 8:17   178
Luke 10:25–37   162, 186
Luke 10:30–37   120
Luke 12:2–3   178
Luke 12:31   180
Luke 14:12–14   162, 186
Luke 14:28–33   196
Luke 15   170
Luke 15:11–24   90
Luke 16:19–31   198
Luke 18:1   206
Luke 18:15   32
Luke 19:1–10   204
Luke 19:10   170
Luke 19:41–44   186
Luke 21:12–19   62
Luke 22:54–62   182
Luke 22:60–62   176
Luke 23:26–49   70
Luke 23:40–43   46

Luke 23:43   106
Luke 24:13–35   152

John

John 1:1–14   76
John 3:16   16, 36, 38, 94,
                         102, 168
John 3:16–21   130
John 3:19   178
John 4:6–29   208
John 4:13–14   28
John 4:27   32
John 4:34   156
John 6:35   208
John 7:37–39   208
John 8:1–11   172
John 8:29   156
John 8:36   46
John 8:44   202
John 9   76
John 9:3   160
John 10:3   32
John 10:10   30
John 13:1–17   124, 162, 188
John 13:34–35   132, 164
John 13:35   42
John 14:3   106
John 14:6–7   76
John 14:13–14   158
John 14:18   180
John 14:24   204
John 14:27   150
John 15:9–12   132
John 15:13   36, 38
John 15:18–27   56
John 16:33   194
John 20:17   88
John 20:23   170
John 20:24–31   80, 210
John 21:1–17   16

Acts

Acts 1:8   60
Acts 2:1–21   82
Acts 2:22–36   70
Acts 2:42–47   42, 96, 122
Acts 2:44   40
Acts 4:13   70
Acts 4:32   40, 96
Acts 4:32–35   42
Acts 7:60   194
Acts 10:28   164
Acts 20:22–24   70
Acts 20:24   52, 60
Acts 20:28   172
Acts 20:35   96, 98
Acts 26:20   20

Romans

Romans 1:11–12   138
Romans 1:20   80
Romans 1:20–32   210
Romans 2:16   178
Romans 3:21–26   94
Romans 3:22–24   102
Romans 3:22–28   46
Romans 4   84
Romans 4:18   78
Romans 5:3–4   62
Romans 5:5   68
Romans 5:6–8   94
Romans 5:8   38, 102, 168
Romans 5:9–11   90
Romans 5:12–19   142
Romans 6:1–4   24
Romans 6:11–14   202
Romans 6:16–23   22, 152
Romans 7:14   202
Romans 8:1–4   75
Romans 8:14–16   88
Romans 8:14–17   12

Romans 8:14–17, 29   190
Romans 8:14–39   162
Romans 8:17–18   62, 100
Romans 8:28   64, 160
Romans 8:31   150
Romans 8:31–32   16
Romans 11:33   208
Romans 12:4–8   156
Romans 12:7   188
Romans 12:8   126
Romans 12:9–10   112
Romans 12:10   42
Romans 12:13   96, 98, 122
Romans 12:14   194
Romans 13:8–10   14
Romans 13:13   118
Romans 14:19   170
Romans 15:7   164, 166

1 Corinthians

1 Corinthians 1:18–31   210
1 Corinthians 2:1–5   126
1 Corinthians 2:6–16   208
1 Corinthians 3:3   118
1 Corinthians 4:1–2   16
1 Corinthians 4:5   178
1 Corinthians 4:12   62
1 Corinthians 4:16   124
1 Corinthians 6:18   178
1 Corinthians 6:20   172
1 Corinthians 7:10–16   14
1 Corinthians 7:23   172
1 Corinthians 9:22   110
1 Corinthians 9:24–27   52
1 Corinthians 10:13   200
1 Corinthians 10:33   110
1 Corinthians 11:1   58, 124
1 Corinthians 11:29–34   66
1 Corinthians 12   16, 156
1 Corinthians 12:14–18   162

1 Corinthians 13   132
1 Corinthians 13:1–3   74
1 Corinthians 13:1–7   164
1 Corinthians 13:4–7   134
1 Corinthians 13:7   18
1 Corinthians 15:19   22
1 Corinthians 15:58   44, 58
1 Corinthians 16:13   194
1 Corinthians 16:13–14   70

2 Corinthians
2 Corinthians 1:3–7   28
2 Corinthians 1:6   62
2 Corinthians 1:8–10   60
2 Corinthians 1:10   34
2 Corinthians 3:1–3   192
2 Corinthians 3:18   190
2 Corinthians 5:7   84
2 Corinthians 5:15   38
2 Corinthians 5:16–19   174
2 Corinthians 5:17   46, 144, 190
2 Corinthians 5:18   168
2 Corinthians 5:18–21   90
2 Corinthians 6:1–2   196
2 Corinthians 6:4   62
2 Corinthians 8:1–5   40
2 Corinthians 8:9   112
2 Corinthians 12:7–10   66
2 Corinthians 12:9–10   60

Galatians
Galatians 1:4   36
Galatians 2:20   144
Galatians 3:26–29   88
Galatians 3:28–29   100
Galatians 4:6–7   88
Galatians 5:1   72, 108
Galatians 5:5   78
Galatians 5:19–21   118
Galatians 5:22–23   120
Galatians 6:7–9   50
Galatians 6:9   58

Ephesians
Ephesians 1:7   94
Ephesians 1:11   162, 190
Ephesians 2:1–6   130, 142
Ephesians 2:4–5   140
Ephesians 2:8–10   102
Ephesians 2:10   108, 162, 190
Ephesians 2:14–18   90
Ephesians 2:19–22   42
Ephesians 3:20   68, 106
Ephesians 4:11–16   16, 156
Ephesians 4:21–24   144
Ephesians 4:22–24   22
Ephesians 4:25   114
Ephesians 4:28   98, 122
Ephesians 4:31–32   20
Ephesians 4:32   170
Ephesians 5:10   156
Ephesians 5:21–33   134
Ephesians 5:25–32   128
Ephesians 5:25–33   136
Ephesians 5:27   192
Ephesians 6:4   18
Ephesians 6:10–18   22, 198
Ephesians 6:12   152

Philippians
Philippians 1   58
Philippians 1:6   108, 160, 162
Philippians 1:20   194
Philippians 1:27   112
Philippians 1:29   62
Philippians 2:1–11   184
Philippians 2:3–4   182
Philippians 2:3–8   188
Philippians 2:12–13   108, 160, 190
Philippians 2:13   162

Philippians 3:1–14   196
Philippians 3:7–14   108
Philippians 3:12–14   92
Philippians 3:12–17   58
Philippians 3:13–14   176
Philippians 4:1   192
Philippians 4:2   124
Philippians 4:6–7   148, 212
Philippians 4:7   150
Philippians 4:10–19   130
Philippians 4:13   34

Colossians
Colossians 1:11   62
Colossians 1:12–14   172
Colossians 1:19–22   90
Colossians 1:21–22   94
Colossians 2:11–12   24
Colossians 3:11   164
Colossians 3:12   120, 186
Colossians 3:13   122, 170
Colossians 3:23–25   156
Colossians 4:2   158
Colossians 4:17   58

1 Thessalonians
1 Thessalonians 1:5   26
1 Thessalonians 1:5–6   124
1 Thessalonians 2:13   26
1 Thessalonians 2:19–20   192
1 Thessalonians 5:10   38

1 Timothy
1 Timothy 1:5   114
1 Timothy 1:12–14   16
1 Timothy 1:15   168
1 Timothy 1:15–16   46
1 Timothy 1:19   114
1 Timothy 2:1–4   158
1 Timothy 2:6   172
1 Timothy 3:16   76

1 Timothy 4:1   82
1 Timothy 4:11–16   58
1 Timothy 4:12   192
1 Timothy 4:14–15   156
1 Timothy 6:6–19   198
1 Timothy 6:12   58
1 Timothy 6:18   98, 188

2 Timothy
2 Timothy 1:5   146
2 Timothy 1:10   28
2 Timothy 2:2   138
2 Timothy 2:3   62
2 Timothy 2:22   86
2 Timothy 3:8   118
2 Timothy 3:12   194
2 Timothy 3:16   26
2 Timothy 4:5   62
2 Timothy 4:16–17   182

Titus
Titus 2:7   58
Titus 3:2   20
Titus 3:3–5   140

Philemon
Philemon 1   130, 138

Hebrews
Hebrews 1:1–2   76
Hebrews 2:18   200
Hebrews 3:6   78
Hebrews 4:12–13   26
Hebrews 4:13   178
Hebrews 4:14–16   212
Hebrews 4:16   140
Hebrews 6:6   118
Hebrews 9:15   172
Hebrews 10:14   36
Hebrews 10:24   124
Hebrews 10:26–27   118
Hebrews 10:35–39   60

Hebrews 10:36   58, 92, 160
Hebrews 11   44, 84
Hebrews 11:1   78, 100
Hebrews 11:1–3   80, 210
Hebrews 11:6   180
Hebrews 12:1–3   44
Hebrews 12:5–11   64
Hebrews 12:5–13   66
Hebrews 12:9   88
Hebrews 12:25   118
Hebrews 13:3   130
Hebrews 13:4   14
Hebrews 13:16   122

James
James 1:1–8   198
James 1:2–4   60, 62
James 1:6–8   158
James 1:13–15   202
James 1:22   74
James 1:27   122
James 2:5   174
James 2:12–13   142
James 2:14–20   74
James 4:4   22
James 4:7   86
James 5:13–16   206
James 5:16   28, 46

1 Peter
1 Peter 1:6–7   64
1 Peter 1:8   84
1 Peter 1:13–21   152
1 Peter 1:18–19   140
1 Peter 1:23   26
1 Peter 2:2–3   208
1 Peter 2:9   72, 108

1 Peter 3:13–22   60
1 Peter 3:18–22   24
1 Peter 4:10   160, 188
1 Peter 4:10–11   16, 156
1 Peter 4:12–13   194
1 Peter 5:3   126
1 Peter 5:8–11   198

2 Peter
2 Peter 1:5–6   208
2 Peter 2:1   172

1 John
1 John 2:9–11   164, 166
1 John 2:15–17   22
1 John 3:1   88, 128
1 John 3:1–3   190
1 John 3:16–18   40, 188
1 John 3:17   98, 122
1 John 3:18   32, 74
1 John 4:7–8   132
1 John 4:9–10   38
1 John 4:19–21   164, 166
1 John 5:14–15   154, 158

Jude
Jude 24   106

Revelation
Revelation 3:19   66
Revelation 5:9   172
Revelation 7:9   164
Revelation 7:9–17   44
Revelation 7:17   106
Revelation 12:11   182
Revelation 14:4   172
Revelation 21:4   106
Revelation 22:12   106

Keywords Index

A

Abiding in Christ 70
Abundant Life 150
Acceptance 12
Accepting Christ 102
Accountability 50
Achievement 146
Adoption 174
Adultery 14, 86
Advent 76
Adversity 60, 70, 78, 130, 150, 194, 206
Affection 128
Affirmation 16, 18
Afterlife 100
Aging 178, 196
Ambition 66, 68, 118, 192, 202
Anger 190, 212
Answers to Prayer 76
Anxiety 150
Apathy 74
Apology 20
Atheism 80
Atonement 38, 172
Attitude 78, 124, 150, 160, 162
Attitudes
    and Emotions 12, 100, 126, 136, 148, 176
Authority of Scripture 26

B

Backsliding 22
Baptism 24
Belief 78, 80, 82, 84, 148, 160, 180, 210
Betrayal 14, 188, 182
Bible 26, 100
Bigotry 54, 164
Bitterness 170
Blessings 154
Boldness 60, 92
Bondage 130, 152, 202
Books 26
Born Again 144
Brokenness 28
Brotherhood 112, 164, 166
Brotherly Love 40, 112, 164, 170
Burdens 28

C

Calling 30, 156, 160, 162
Career 114, 146, 190, 192
Caring 32, 42, 96, 98, 164
Challenges 34, 60, 92
Character 114, 164, 178
Cheerfulness 150
Childlike Faith 160
Child Rearing 40
Children 14, 18, 68, 70, 140, 146, 194

Choices   54, 86, 108, 114,
                        182, 196
Christian   144
Christian Life   32, 74, 144, 150
Christlikeness   32
Christ the Burden Bearer   36
Christ the Only Savior   36
Christ the Substitute
   for Humanity   36, 38
Christmas   68, 76, 140, 168
Christ's Forgiveness   168
Christ's Love   28, 36, 102,
                        128, 168
Church   16, 40, 42, 72,
                    96, 122, 188
Church as the Family of God   42
Church Involvement   74
Circumstances and Faith   78, 160
Comfort   22, 28
Comforter   150
Commandments   50
Commitment   14, 54, 58, 164
Communication   124
Community   32, 40, 42, 96,
                98, 112, 122, 124,
                132, 138, 164, 188
Companionship   64
Compassion   28, 42, 96,
                    98, 164, 172
Competition   156
Complacency   44
Compromise   54, 114, 176, 178
Confession   20, 46, 116
Confidence   78, 126, 160
Conflict   20, 70, 124, 170, 182
Confrontation   124
Conscience   48, 114, 178
Consequences   50, 176
Consideration   98
Contentment   150

Convenience   22
Conversion   46, 144, 148, 172
Convictions   52, 54, 112, 164
Cooperation   124
Courage   56, 58, 60, 70, 92,
               110, 112, 116, 148,
               164, 170, 194, 198
Cowardice   54
Crime   46, 176
Cross   38, 100
Curiosity   208

D

Darkness   178
Death   38, 46, 58, 148,
                        164, 180
Death to Sin   24
Deceit   48
Deception   48, 178, 202
Decisions   108, 196
Dedication   58
Deliverance   28, 64
Dependence on God   34, 60, 70
Desire   154, 170, 196
Desires   68
Despair   94, 100, 130,
                    148, 176, 206
Desperation   206
Destiny   108, 160, 162, 176
Determination   62, 170
Devil   200
Devotion   38, 52, 56, 58, 96
Difficulties   78, 84, 92, 206
Dignity   190
Diligence   44
Disabilities   24, 160, 190
Disappointments   68
Discernment   152
Disciples   72
Discipleship   26, 74, 138, 192

Discipline 64, 66
Discouragement 150
Dishonor 182
Disobedience 154
Divine Help 76
Divorce 88
Doubt 76, 78, 80, 104, 160, 180
Dreams 68, 196
Dying to Self 24, 188

E

Earnestness in Prayer 212
Encouragement 16, 18
Endurance 62
Enemies 70, 122, 142
Envy 118
Eternal Life 106
Eternal Perspective 106
Evangelism 32, 34, 60, 72, 110
Evil 38, 198
Evil Desire 22
Example 58, 74
Expectations 68
Expedience 22
Experience 80
Experiencing God 76, 80, 104

F

Failure 176, 196
Faith 34, 60, 78, 80, 82, 84, 92, 104, 148, 160, 180, 194, 210
Faithfulness 14, 16, 56, 60, 86, 156, 178, 198
False Doctrine 82
False Gods 82
False Religions 82
False Teaching 82
Fame 192, 202

Family 14, 18, 42, 70, 88, 96, 134, 140, 164, 168, 170, 180, 192, 194
Family of God 12
Fatherhood 14, 18, 88, 146
Fatherhood of God 12, 88, 90, 174, 180
Fathers 14, 18, 70, 90, 146, 164, 180
Faultfinding 20
Fear 16, 34, 54, 64, 70, 92, 138, 148
Fear of God 64
Fellowship 96
Forgiveness 20, 24, 46, 94, 122, 140, 142, 168, 170, 172
Forsaking God 104
Freedom 24, 36, 72, 130, 142, 150
Friendship 40, 42, 96, 124, 130, 138
Fruit 192
Fruitfulness 192
Frustration 68, 192
Future 176

G

Generosity 40, 96, 98, 120, 188
Gift of Salvation 102, 106
Giving 40, 96, 98, 110, 120, 164
Goals 192, 196
God the Creator 174, 210
God's Faithfulness 64
God's Goodness 64, 102
God's Love 128
God's Mercy 140
God's Will 64, 68, 158, 160

God's Wrath 140
Gospel 100
Grace 46, 94, 102, 106, 122, 140, 142, 172, 194, 204
Gratitude 130
Great Commission 34
Greed 66, 198
Grief 90, 164
Growth 16, 138, 204
Guidance 64, 196
Guilt 48, 94, 114

H

Happiness 14
Hardness of Heart 118
Hardship 62, 66, 104
Harvest 192
Hatred 70, 166
Healing 28
Heaven 90, 100, 106
Help from God 34, 108, 206
Holiness 178
Homelessness 42
Honesty 114, 116, 178, 212
Hope 68, 78, 94, 100, 148, 196
Human Help 40, 96, 98, 122, 130, 164
Human Love 128
Human Nature 154
Human Will 68, 154, 158
Human Worth 110, 174, 186
Humility 126
Husbands 134, 136
Hypocrisy 54

I

Identity in Christ 12, 144
Ideologies and Belief Systems 80

Image of God 30
Incarnation 76
Individualism 162
Indwelling of Christ 144
Influence 58
Injustice 112, 130, 164
Insignificance 162
Inspiration of Persons 30
Integrity 114, 116, 178, 198

J

Jealousy 118
Jesus Christ 76, 100
Joy 156
Judgment 50
Justice 26, 112, 130, 142

K

Kindness 120, 122
Knowledge 208
Knowledge and Knowing 152

L

Law 142
Leadership 58, 112, 124, 126, 166, 192
Leadership of the Church 126
Learning 138, 208
Legacy 164, 192
Light 178
Loneliness 138, 148, 180
Losing 52
Loss 58, 66, 164, 190, 196
Love 18, 32, 36, 40, 42, 46, 66, 70, 96, 98, 120, 122, 130, 132, 134, 136, 148, 166, 188, 204
Love for Enemies 194
Loyalty 38, 56, 96, 130
Lust 178
Lying 48, 114

M

Marriage 14, 86, 134, 136, 178
Materialism 66
Meaning of Life 12, 30, 52, 80, 132, 146, 162
Men 14, 86, 136, 178, 190
Mentor 26
Mentoring 26, 132, 138, 192
Mercy 46, 94, 122, 140, 142, 172
Middle Age 178
Mind 208
Ministry 16, 34, 44, 60, 74, 110, 120, 126, 148, 156, 164, 188, 192
Miracles 82, 104
Mission 30, 192
Missionary 60, 156
Missions 60, 110, 156
Mistakes 176
Money 40, 96, 98, 110, 198
Morality 50
Mothers 70, 140
Motivation 204
Mystery 208, 210

N

Need 98
New Age 82
New Life 24, 144, 172
New Man 144, 172

O

Obedience 60, 154, 204
Occult 82
Old Man 22
Opportunity 176, 196
Oppression 130
Optimism 78
Orphans 180
Overcoming 34, 78, 92, 150

P

Pain 28, 62
Paradise 106
Parenting 18, 40, 88, 146
Parents 136
Passover 140
Past 108
Peace 148, 150, 168
Peacemakers 170
Perception and Reality 152
Persecution 56, 70, 194
Perseverance 22, 58, 60, 62, 170, 194
Pessimism 78
Planning 154
Plans 154
Pleasing God 156
Possessions 110
Prayer 70, 76, 104, 148, 154, 158, 180, 194, 212
Prayer for Enemies 194
Prayer in God's Will 158
Predestination 108
Prejudice 70, 164
Presence of God 76
Pressure 194
Pride 20, 118, 190
Principles 52
Priorities 146, 182, 196
Prisons 26, 46, 130, 150
Problems 78, 206
Protection 150
Providence 160
Purity 86, 178
Purpose 30, 52, 58, 72, 108, 160, 162, 176, 188, 190, 194
Pursuing God 208

Q

Questions   208
Quitting   58, 196

R

Race Relations   26
Racism   54, 70, 112, 124,
               130, 164, 166
Raising Children   146
Rebellion   154
Rebuke   126
Reconciliation   20, 90, 124, 166,
                    168, 170
Redeemer   172
Redemption   26, 38, 94, 130,
                 172, 174, 176
Regeneration   172
Regret   46, 90, 94, 176
Rejection   14, 190
Relationships   26, 32, 42, 90,
                 124, 128, 130,
           138, 168, 170, 192
Religion   82
Renewal   150
Renewing the Mind   150
Repentance   46, 108, 172, 204
Rescue   130
Responsibility   16
Rest   106
Results   192
Resurrection   100
Righteousness by Faith   102
Risk   16, 84
Role Models   26
Roles   30
Romance   128, 136
Romantic Love   128

S

Sabbath   52

Sacrifice   36, 38, 52, 58,
              110, 112, 124, 164,
                 172, 184, 188
Salvation   24, 36, 46, 140, 172
Salvation by Grace   102
Sanctification   204
Satan   22, 198, 200, 202
Savior   28
Science   80, 104, 210
Scripture   26
Second Chances   16, 170
Secrets   178
Security in God   150
Seduction   198
Seeking God   104, 180
Seen and Unseen   84, 152
Self-Denial   86
Self-Exaltation   68
Self-Image   186
Selfishness   14, 50, 66, 118,
                 124, 134, 182, 188
Selflessness   184
Self-Reliance   82, 188
Self-Sacrifice   36, 96, 98, 134
Self-Sufficiency   50, 132, 134
Self-Will   154
Self-Worth   12, 162, 186, 190
Separation   90, 180
Servanthood   120, 162, 188
Service   44, 74, 132, 156,
                 164, 184, 188
Sex   14, 178
Sexual Immorality   178
Shame   24, 176
Sharing   40
Significance   12, 162, 176,
                     186, 190
Signs and Wonders   104
Silence   206
Sin   14, 24, 46, 50, 86, 116,
             118, 170, 200, 202

Sinful Pleasure 22
Skepticism 104, 160, 210
Slavery 24, 152, 202
Social Action 54
Sorrow 28, 46, 164
Sowing and Reaping 50, 176, 192
Spiritual Bondage 24
Spiritual Death 46
Spiritual Desire 208
Spiritual Formation 16, 138, 204
Spiritual Gifts 16, 44, 156
Spiritual Growth 138
Spiritual Hunger 180, 208
Spiritual Thirst 208
Spiritual Warfare 22, 152
Sports 124, 156, 190
Steadfastness 70
Stewardship 16
Strength 58, 62, 70, 108, 194
Stress 194
Submission 158
Success 146, 190, 196
Suffering 28, 62, 100
Supernatural Experiences 82
Support 40
Surrender 52
Suspicion 102

T

Teachers 74, 192
Teamwork 124, 166
Teenagers 138, 192
Temptation 22, 86, 116, 178, 198, 200, 202
Ten Commandments 14, 50
Thoughts 150
Time 146
Transformation 204
Trials 34, 194, 206

Trust 34, 60, 78, 84, 126, 158, 160, 210
Trustworthiness of God 84
Truth 22, 116, 152, 178, 208

U

Unanswered Prayer 206
Unbelief 102, 104, 148, 180, 210
Uncertainties 84
Unconditional Love 122
Unfaithfulness 14, 178
Unity 112, 124, 166
Unselfishness 98, 184, 188

V

Values 110
Vanity 118
Victory 78
Visible and Invisible 84
Vocation 190, 196
Vows 14

W

War 72
Weakness 160, 190
Weddings 136
Winning 52
Wisdom 30, 132, 196, 208
Wives 134
Women 14, 208
Work 114, 146, 162, 190, 192, 196
Works 102
World 22, 152
Wrestling with God 212

Y

Youth 130, 138, 192

Notes

Notes

Notes

Notes

Notes

Notes

Notes

Notes

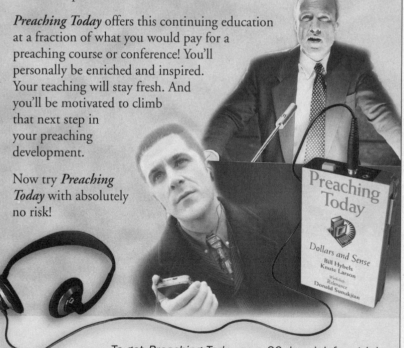

We want to hear from you. Please send your comments about this book to us in care of zreview@zondervan.com. Thank you.

GRAND RAPIDS, MICHIGAN 49530 USA

WWW.ZONDERVAN.COM